GHOSTS ARE REAL:

Proof of the Paranormal

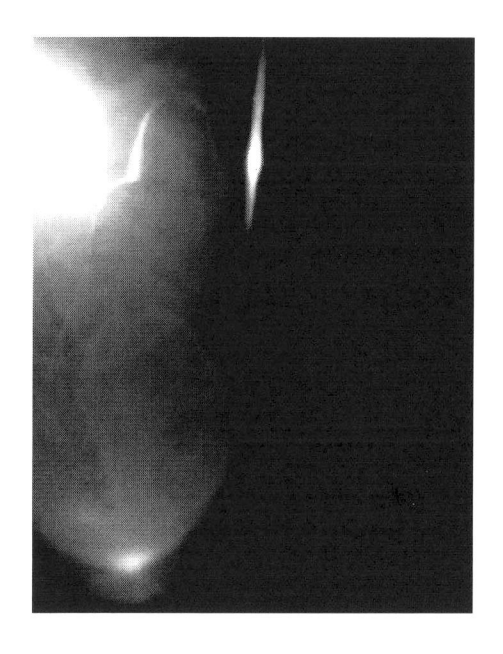

Real stories of the paranormal

Written by Peter Kanellis

Copyright © 2019 by Peter Kanellis

All rights reserved.

No part of this publication may be reproduced, distributed, or transmitted in any form or by any means, including photocopying, recording, or other electronic or mechanical methods, without the prior written permission of the publisher, except in the case of brief quotations embodied in critical reviews and certain other noncommercial uses permitted by copyright law. For permission requests, write to the publisher, addressed "Attention: Permissions Coordinator," at PO Box 4631 Ithaca, NY 14852.

Front cover image by Peter Kanellis.

All rights reserved for the "Warning" painting by artist Gabrielle O'Neill. Medium: water paint. 2019.

ISBN: 9781707050390

Find Ghost Hunters of the Finger Lakes on Facebook.

This book is dedicated to the family and friends who have inspired and encouraged me to write.

INTRODUCTION

At the early age of nine year's old, I would listen to my grandmother's ghost stories and how she could actually see spirits. I didn't know it at the time but she instilled in me a fascination of the paranormal. Having paranormal activity in my grandmother's home and listening to family members tell me the things that could not be explained led me to investigate and research the paranormal. I wanted to try to capture real ghost in photos and gather real evidence of the paranormal. I did not want to follow the same path as most paranormal researchers but to try different methods of researching and capturing real paranormal evidence. Using dowsing rods and different camera equipment seemed to work for me. Also growing up with a sensitive grandmother and having our own personal paranormal stories seemed to help us during our investigations after we founded the Ghost Hunters of the Finger Lakes. Our cases have led us to many interesting and fascinating places.

Born and raised in Upstate NY I have always enjoyed fishing and hiking in the beautiful gorges and trails in the Finger Lakes region. I have also found there are many historic sites in Upstate NY. There were many so-called Indian trails/burial grounds and campsites where Native Americans once resided. Also the well-known Harriet Tubman and the connected Underground Railroads and connecting escape routes can be found in the surrounding area. Many small towns with historic sites, such as the Erie Canal, where towns were built due to the easy access through the water ways exist as well. I should not leave out the Civil War and the Revolutionary War, both of which left behind high amounts of energy from the battles and very gruesome deaths. I believe the impact of the battles and deaths seemed to stay with and imprinted within the land and areas where these events played out long ago. Some people can actually still feel the energy left behind. Others have actually witnessed these events still going on to this day.

I will share some of my grandma's personal ghost stories and some of my own spirit photos from my paranormal investigations. Again, certain names and identifying characteristics have been changed for anonymity. Photos may be cropped to remove the people in my stories, but otherwise remain unaltered.

If you like reading ghost stories or like investigating haunted places this book is for you. The following stories are from some of my past paranormal investigations but the names and details of events have been changed to protect the identities of those involved. I also include stories of near death experiences, inhuman entities and how people and their families can have paranormal experiences as they are close to death. I offer some self-protection techniques that may help you stay shielded and protected from negative energy.

MY GRANDMA'S STORIES

At nine years old I never thought much about my grandmother's stories or why she could see ghosts. I just thought that what she did was interesting and I wanted to hear her stories. It did not occur to me at the time that her ghost stories were real when she would be having actual spirit encounters.

I would often stay overnight at my grandma's house. It was a very old house built in the 1900s. I remember that my grandma's beds were really big and she had really thick feather beds on top of them. I would often sink deep into the feather beds as my grandma would turn the lights off. Sunk deep into the pillow beds and not really being able to move, my eyes would widen as I would wait for my grandmother to tell me her ghost stories.

Back in the 1900s there was no technology or equipment to capture paranormal activity so many experiences were passed on through story-telling. These ghost stories my grandmother told me were nonetheless true and very real.

My grandmother is on the right and my grandmother's friend, Ray, is on the left side of the photo. Both of them were gifted with psychic abilities. Ray will be featured in many of my grandma's stories.

MAN IN THE TOP HAT

When my grandma was around sixteen years old, she started seeing a man standing by the foot of her bed at night. She knew that something about the man was not quite right. He was dressed in a black suit and had a large black top hat on his head. Usually this spirit man would just appear out of nowhere and stand right by my grandma's bed staring at her. She would think, "Why is this man standing by my bed at night and what does he want?" When she would see the man in the top hat she would scream out as loud as she could. Not knowing who or why this man was there really frightened her. Her parents would come running to her room and ask, "What's wrong?" Many times the spirit man would disappear by walking through her bedroom wall. Sometimes he would disappear by walking through her bedroom window! The window was very high off the ground because my grandma's bedroom was on the second floor. If this man had been human he would have fallen to the ground and been very badly hurt, if not killed by the impact from the fall. My grandma often wondered why she could see this man but her parents would never see him. She also wondered, "What does this spirit man want and why is he bothering me at night?"

Then, one night everything changed, and grandma said that she would never forget it. The spirit man in the top hat appeared to her and walked over by the end of her bed. He leaned down over her by her feet. This made my grandma very nervous as she always slept with her feet sticking out of the covers. She did not like to cover them up with the blankets. As the spirit man continued to stare at my grandma he reached out and grabbed my grandma's toes! What really spooked her was that the man in the top hat's fingers felt ice cold and they shot a chill through her when he touched her. When this happened my grandma started screaming as loud as she could! The man in the top hat just slowly walked out of her room and walked right past her parents as they walked in to check on her. This was the last time grandma would see the spirit man in the suit and top hat.

      I thought this was a pretty cool and scary story, but I was left with more questions than answers. While telling another psychic medium about the man in the top hat, the psychic medium told me she thought that the spirit was one of grandma's spirit guides. Another psychic thought he may have been an actual man that lived in the community and died nearby. But that is all I really know of the man in the top hat. This sparked my interest in the Afterlife and what lies beyond the realms of what most people cannot see or even imagine.

HORSE AND CART STORY

My grandma was only four years old when she started having psychic visions and premonitions. One day my grandma was playing downstairs in the living room area at her home. All of a sudden she heard the sound of horses riding toward her house. She ran over and looked out the front window to see who it was in the front yard. She could see a man sitting on a cart with two horses pulling it. The man looked sad, and one of the horses appeared hurt as the horse limped on his right leg. Grandma knew right away that something was wrong, so she yelled out for her mother to come over and look out the front window. When her mom looked out the window, nothing was there. Grandma said, "Can't you see the horse and cart? Oh, and by the way, one of our relatives is dead. A man is going to tell you about the death very soon."

Her mother scolded her and told her to go to her room: "Don't ever say stuff like that ever again!" she said. Grandma could not figure out why her mother could not see the horse and cart and why she was unaware about the death of her family member. As Grandma lay in her bed very confused and thinking about what had just happened, the mother heard the sound of horses riding up to the house. She looked out the front door and noticed that one of the horses was limping on his right front leg. The man riding on the cart looked very sad. She knew by the look on the man's face he did not have good news for her.

As she opened the front door the man looked at her and

said, "I have some very bad news for you. Your grandma passed away and it appears she had a heart attack." Her grandmother had had no illnesses or any warning indicating that she would die of a heart attack so there was no way that anyone could have predicted that she would have died that day. The mother looked back at her daughter and now knew that she was gifted and understood that she was different from the rest of her children.

My grandma's ghost stories always stuck with me, even today as I am writing this book. She also had stories about how she would see things before they would actually happen. She also knew who the person was on the other end of the phone when it would ring. She realized at a very young age that not everyone could see or do what she could so she kept quiet about her gift, telling very few people what she could do. I do not think she really understood her gift and never quite fully developed it.

PREMONITION OF DEATH

My grandma told me a story about one of the premonitions that she had later on in life. One day my grandma thought she would lie down and take a nap as she was very tired. As she was sleeping, she had a very bad feeling and quickly sat up in bed. My grandma could see burning flames shooting out of the end of her bed. As she looked closer she could see a face begin to appear in the flames. She knew right away something was wrong as she could now see in detail whose face it was.

It was her brother's face in the burning fire at the end of her bed. She quickly jumped out of bed and tried calling around to find out what happened to him. She sensed it was not good.

My grandma learned that her brother had just died in a very bad automobile accident. Back then there were no seatbelts so cars were very unsafe. I am unsure if the car caught on fire when the accident occurred but it was at the same time the accident was taking place that Grandma had the vision telling her that her brother was actually killed in a bad car accident.

I thought it must be very scary having visions like this. I am not sure I would want to ever see them. At the same time I wondered why she was given these visions. Was it a warning? Or possibly she was so open to the spirit world she could sense when something bad was going to happen. Her psychic intuition helped her reveal things that most people would think impossible.

LOST EYE GLASSES

Later on in life Grandma would meet a man named Ray who was a very gifted psychic medium. Word got out that Ray and my grandma helped people find their lost personal items. One day a man stopped by and asked if grandma would help him find his eye glasses in a cornfield. He really needed them and hoped Grandma or Ray could help him out. My grandma said, "We will try to help you out. But you lost them in a cornfield?"

"Yes," the man said.

"I will see what I can do." Grandma said. Later that day Grandma and Ray stopped over to the man's farm. The man was out in his field working, so Ray walked out to the corn field. He stopped and looked around because he noticed a chair out in the field and was drawn to it.

Ray walked over and sat down in the chair thinking about the man's glasses. Suddenly and without even looking, Ray reached up into the cornstalk behind his head and pulled the man's glasses off of them.

"Here you go! I found them for you." Ray said as he happily returned the glasses to the man. The man was shocked and said, "Wow! That's pretty impressive. It isn't easy finding eye glasses in a cornfield! How did you do that?"

"I'm not sure. It just comes to me and I just know things and where they are." Ray said.

Personal objects can hold energy so it is possible that he sought after the energy and it seemed to help guide him to these objects, but this is just another one of my theories behind energy.

THE MISSING WALLET

A family friend stopped by to see Grandma one day and looked very upset. He had lost his wallet and had no idea where he had lost it. He had just gotten paid and had his whole week's salary in it. It was a lot of money and during a time when money was hard to come by, so the young man asked Grandma if she could help him find the wallet. "Well we will try and help you," she said. "Give us a week and Ray and I will see what we can do."

The next night Ray had a vision of what happened to the man's wallet. Ray did not want to get anyone in trouble but did mention that someone had stolen the wallet and he knew who it was. "I don't want to cause problems." Ray said. He offered to use transference to send my grandmother visions and see if she could get the message of where the wallet was. Grandma told the young man to come back in a week to see if she had gotten any information about his wallet.

That week Grandma started to have visions of a man. She saw a man's face in her house mirrors. When she was driving her car she would see a man's face appear in her car rearview mirror. She would get out and walk around the car to see if there was actually a man standing behind the car but she would not find anyone near it. Finally at the end of the week, she figured out what was going on. She also knew who this man was as she had seen him before.

The man who lost his wallet stopped back to see what they had found out. "I know who this man is as I had many visions." Grandma said. "You know him too. You were in the store last week and you dropped your wallet on the floor. A man walked up behind you and scooped up the wallet before you knew it was missing. He waited until you walked away. He works at the store. If you go back there you can ask him for your wallet back."

She told him the man's name and told him to go back to the store and ask him about his wallet. "Okay," the young man said, "I will let you know what happens."

The next day the young man returned to grandma's house to tell her what happened. He shared, "I went to the store and looked for the man you told me had my wallet. He was in the store stocking shelves and he nervously looked over at me when I walked toward him. I straight out asked him if he had found a wallet that had money in it. 'In fact, someone told me you have my wallet!' I said. The man had a shocked look on his face and admitted to having it. 'But how did you know that?' he asked. The man said, 'You dropped the wallet on the floor and no one else was around so I picked it up and put it in my pocket.' I told him that I have my ways of knowing things." The man was appreciative and did not want to get Grandma in trouble for helping him to get his wallet back.

LOST DIAMOND RING

One day a lady stopped by my grandma's house and mentioned that she had lost a very special diamond ring. She looked everywhere for it but it was nowhere to be found. Ray was there with Grandma and said, "I know where it is. You would never think to look for it there."

The lady looked puzzled. "Really?" she asked? "Where do you think the ring is?"

Ray said, "When you washed your dishes in a large pan of water your ring slipped off your finger and fell into the pan. After that happened, you tossed out the water in the yard. That's where you will find your ring. It's lying out in your front yard." Ray continued to tell the lady exactly where the ring was located in the yard lying next to her walkway.

The lady said, "I do wash my dishes in a large pan and that may have actually happened."

"It's in the front yard. Just look for the ring and it will be there." Ray said.

Sure enough when the lady looked in her front yard where she threw the water out, the ring was laying right by the walkway. The lady was really happy to get her diamond ring back as it meant a lot to her. Once again, Ray was using his gift to help those around him.

THE ROCKING CHAIR

One day my mom was telling me about my grandma's old rocking chair. My grandma loved to sit in that chair and just rock back and forth. Ray would also use the rocking chair when he connected with spirits. Ray would go into a trance state while sitting in the rocking chair to receive messages from the Other Side. Ray said that he had a Native American guide who would help him by giving him messages that he needed to hear.

Years after Ray and my grandma had passed away our family had inherited my grandma's home. Many of my grandparents' possessions were still in the house, yet to be discovered. After looking around the house I actually found the rocking chair upstairs in the attic. However, the arm and leg were broken and needed to be reattached. As I continued to look around, I also found the other wooden leg for the bottom part of the rocking chair. I reattached the leg to the rocking chair. It almost seemed like I was getting helped by some unknown force because it went back together very fast and seemed to rock perfectly afterwards. I took the rocking chair down to my mom's house and showed her the rocking chair. She was reminded of stories about the chair and how grandma loved it. I left the chair in my mom's living room and returned home for the night.

Later that night, my mom heard noises coming from the living room area. She was nervous as she did not have any pets and it was just her alone in the house since my father had passed away. She looked over to where the rocking chair was sitting and she noticed that the chair was rocking back and forth very quickly. She walked toward the chair and as she got closer, the chair stopped rocking abruptly. She looked around to see if any of the windows were open or if there was someone messing with her, but there was no one in the room.

I would like to believe that either Ray or Grandma were trying out the rocking chair one last time.

This is my grandma's rocking chair, the same chair in which Ray would sit and channel spirits. When we were younger we would sit in this chair, close our eyes, and try to see spirits like Ray. We never had any luck doing it. One psychic told me there was a lot of energy still attached to the chair. Which made sense as the chair was used as a tool to channel spirits. One thing I have learned over the years is objects can hold energy, both positive and negative which means they can even be haunted the same way people or houses can.

MY GRANDMA'S HOUSE

Many years later, my grandma's house seemed to hold onto a lot of energy, so when family members lived in the house they would start having unexplained events happen to them that they could not understand. My sister, for instance, had many experiences while staying at our grandma's house that will forever stay with her.

One night, my sister, Patti, had washed some dishes and stored them in the drainer next to the sink to dry. She went to bed as usual. However, the next morning when she looked at the kitchen sink, she could see dishes stacked up in it. She knew she had put the dishes in the drainer the night before and could not figure how they had been stacked up like that in the sink. They were also positioned in a very abnormal way: There was a frying pan with a plate on it. Then a glass was placed upside down on the plate. Then, there was some silverware on top of the glass, which was really strange. My sister knew that she was alone in the house at the time of this happening so she knew that no one could have been messing with her.

Another time Patti said she was taking a bath and she could hear something in the bathroom with her. All of a sudden she heard a loud thud outside the tub on the bathroom floor. She paused a second then she threw open the shower curtains to see what was there in the bathroom with her. It was very strange that no one was there but she could see a bottle of shampoo in the middle of the bathroom floor. "How in the hell did that get there?" she said out loud. The shampoo bottle was not even near the area it was placed; it had to be moved from one area to another. Having objects moving around while you are taking a bath sounds very terrifying but she was used to weird things happening there in her house.

It reminded me of another story my sister told me about her library room as she called it. My sister loves to read and has a huge collection of books in this one room. One morning Patti got out of bed and starting walking down the hallway towards her library room. She started to notice books had been placed out in the hallway and opened up to a standing V and sitting upward. I always wondered what the books titles were and what the spirits trying to tell her. Or, were the spirits only being playful. Either way, it would take a lot of energy to move objects around like that.

Another time, Patti was up late after working odd hours as a nurse. At about three o'clock in the morning, she heard a loud click in an upstairs bedroom. She was nervous and thought someone had broken into her house. When she looked around she did not see anyone and all of her doors were still locked. She proceeded to the upstairs and found that a camp light was on. It was an older push button style camp lantern, so she needed to push the button down fairly hard to get it to turn off. She walked over to it and clicked the light off, then she went to bed for the night.

My sister has had this happen to her a few times now. She recently had a camp light turn on just before we went on one of our investigations for Ghost Hunters of the Finger Lakes. The camp light had been positioned on the floor by her front entry door. When I arrived at her house to pick her up, she said, "You just missed it. My camp light just clicked on by itself a couple of minutes ago."

As I had gotten further into investigating the paranormal, I approached incidences with a more skeptic attitude in order to find rational explanations for activity. In this instance, I checked the camp light by pushing the button switch on and off. I shook it and tried to get it to turn on without pushing the buttons in case the batteries had a faulty connection allowing the energy to come and go. There was no way that this lamp could have turned on by itself so something or someone would have had to have pushed the button to turn it on. Patti just laughed and said, "I told you something had turned it on. My ghosts are friendly and just let me know they are around by turning things on once in a while."

Another night Patti was asleep upstairs in my grandma's old house. Suddenly a noise started coming from one of the rooms upstairs. She became nervous because she was alone in the house and again feared that someone had broken in. It was also on Halloween night so she thought someone was playing around or playing tricks on her.

The noise was getting louder. When she walked into the room she found a very old radio in a bedroom Patti used for storage. The sound was the radio playing music. This radio was easily thirty years old and had not been used in many years. When my sister checked the radio she found that it was not plugged into an outlet. Patti called me and told me about the radio turning on, so I came over to investigate. Again, approaching the situation with skepticism and rational thinking,

I examined the batteries that were in the back of it. The batteries were so corroded that they had to be at least twenty years old. They were also fused together so there was little chance that the radio could have been working, let alone playing music. Why did it just turn on after so many years of being in storage? We still do not have the answer to this.

The batteries were clearly corroded and did not even make contact with the circuit. I tried to get the radio to work, but as you can see for yourself, there is a good reason why the radio would not play for me. I was very fascinated by this and wanted to know why unexplained events were happening in my grandma's old house. Were there spirits turning on the radio for some reason? Were they trying to tell us something was going to happen? One thing we did connect to the activity is one of our family members were sick at the time of this so maybe it was connected in some way, but that is all we can figure out of why electronic devices were being turned on at that point in time.

I was pretty intrigued by the radio incident and will never forget how curious I was to learn that there were no reasonable answers for all the activity going on in the house. A medium once told us that there was a little Native American spirit girl in my sister's house and that she liked to play around with electrical items and objects there. She said Native Americans lived nearby there at one point and there were even burial grounds near the house.

When checking for Native American land in the area, I found a map backing-up what this medium had told us. I also found a historic sign, showing that "Indians and early settlers" would go there for the salt in the stream outside at the back of the house. This evidence also matched up to what Ray would say about one of his guides being a Native American.

Another family member that stayed at grandma's house had some paranormal experiences, too. He would start hearing loud noises upstairs at night. At first he tried to ignore the noises by turning up the sound to the TV but the noise got so loud that it sounded like someone was dragging furniture across the floor upstairs and throwing it in a big pile. He would just look up at the ceiling and wonder, "What the hell is making so much noise?" However, when he checked upstairs there was nothing out of place and no indication that anything had been moved.

These types of activity in my grandmother's home (now my sister's) combined with my grandmother's stories shared during my childhood sparked my curiosity in the paranormal. I began conducting research through books, articles, and anecdotes. I also started testing items like dowsing rods and ways to communicate with spirits. Story telling was used to share paranormal activity, but technology has helped shift the way society thinks about ghost stories through the use of scientific investigation and documentation through newly invented equipment.

DOWSING RODS

This led me to testing different kinds of paranormal equipment for detecting energy. I do not mean electrical energy as there are plenty of ways to detect that. Energy in this context is related to static magnetic energy. Some people are able to feel or sense these static charges. The most common response people notice may be having the hairs stand straight up on their arms or neck.

One of the tools for detecting or communicating with this type of energy would be dowsing. I was curious about how dowsing worked and how dowsing methods could detect energy. Some dowsers would use crystal pendulums that would circle in a clockwise motion indicating "yes" or counter clockwise for "no." The pendulum could also swing sideways or like a north/south direction, depending on what the dowser asked it. One medium I have worked with would use a pendulum over a person's body to check their energy chakras and see what areas she needed to focus on.

Another form of dowsing was used to find water with a forked wooden stick. The dowser would walk until the stick was pulled to the ground, showing the location of a water vein. This art form is also known as "witching for water." Some people still practice this art and have a lot of success with it. When my well was drilled for my house 30 years ago, the well driller had a man walk my land and mark the best area to drill for water. He used the forked stick method and found a good spot to increase his chances of finding a good water vein. When his workers drilled the well, they hit a large water vein at 28 feet down right away. The well driller said, "There's no need to drill anymore as there is plenty of water for your house." I remembered how impressed I was by all this. How can a man walk around with a stick and find water under the ground with it? I later learned that water is energy and the sticks or rods would search out the energy and point to it. I believe that the person using the rods or sticks are the actual vessels being used to find water or energy. Not everyone can do this; I believe you have to be gifted in some way.

This piqued my interest so much that I wanted to make my own set of dowsing rods to experiment with knowing that wood was not the only material used for this purpose. I read that you could find energy and spirits with copper or metal dowsing rods, so I was very eager. My first set of dowsing rods was pretty simple. I took a coat hanger and cut it in half and bent some handles so I could hold them out in front of me. The coat hanger rods would not move as I held them out and ask them to move or point to energy in the room. One day, we were going to my grandmother's old house. One of my family members asked, "Why don't you bring the dowsing rods to grandma's house? If they are going to work, it will be at grandma's house."

It made sense, so I tried the dowsing rods out in my grandmother's living room (now my sister Patti's living room). I was shocked by what happened: the metal rods started to slowly spin in my hands. Then the rods started spinning faster and faster and then, so fast that they were almost like helicopter blades. They spun so fast I had to hold them away from my face. I could feel the energy shoot through my body as the hair on my arms stood straight up. After that day, my dowsing rods have always worked for me and with great accuracy.

I updated my dowsing rods from the rudimentary first attempt, and continued making different kinds. I like copper as it seems to be a good conductor for picking up energy. I still love the different terms people use for my dowsing rods. They have been referred to as waddle sticks, stick things, magic sticks, or

Ouija sticks. They are helpful because I can quickly dowse a house and locate hot spots or where the spirit energy is at. This helps the Ghost Hunters of the Finger Lakes team locate hot spots as we set up our equipment, and helps to determine where to point the trail cameras.

I also have a lighted set of dowsing rods as they let you see and dowse in dark locations. I can get answers to "yes" and "no" questions in the dark this way. Usually, the families want to ask what spirits are in the house with them. One bed and breakfast place I started dowsing at really proved that the rods were right on. Not knowing much history about the house, I started to dowse and ask where the spirits wanted me to go. They led me upstairs to a small bedroom. I asked if it was a man or woman whom had led me there. There was no response, so I asked if a child had led me there. My dowsing rods crossed for "yes." I asked if there was a boy there. The rods swung outward for "no." Then I asked if it was a young girl and they quickly crossed in for a "yes."

The owner of the bed and breakfast was watching very intently as I dowsed. I started asking for the age of the young girl. I got down to ages between eight and ten years old, but before I could ask for the exact age, the owner blurted out "Oh, my God! Yes! A young nine year old girl who was very sick died in that bed there."

She knew the history of the house very well, but she said that no one really knew about the death because it was not known to many people. Right as the owner mentioned the little girl dying in the bed, my EMF meter, which I had laid on the bed, started to go off. (This is more information on EMF meters to come.) We got a very high EMF reading where the little girl had died. It was the only time that the meter spiked in the bedroom and we could not get it to it to go off again.

Later on people wanted to ask my dowsing rods questions. I was kind of hesitant at first. One lady asked them if one of her relatives would be pregnant soon. My rods quickly crossed for "yes!" She asked again, "Is she pregnant now?" There was another quick cross for "yes" again!

"No way!" the lady said. "She told me yesterday she cannot get pregnant. She just told me that!" She was arguing with my dowsing rods it was quite funny, but unnerving at the same time.

I just stated, "Hey, I don't control what they say."

The lady looked mad and stated "Those damn things don't work," and she stopped asking questions. Then she said, "I will find out the truth tonight! I *will* ask her if she is pregnant or not."

I thought, "Oh great. I don't need this," but at the same time I was curious if the dowsing rods were accurate or not. The next day the lady had a funny look on her face as she approached me. She told me, "I asked her if she was pregnant or not and guess what? Those things were right! She is four months pregnant and she did not want to tell anyone yet so she was keeping it quiet. Those damn stick things do work!" Then she wanted to ask more questions of course.

Much of the time, the dowsing rods were right. I quit doing "yes" and "no" questions about such topics not related to the investigation though after some more events. One question was if they were going to be divorced or not? The rods said "Yes" and they later ended up in a divorce like the dowsing rods had predicted. I did not like the idea of ending up in some divorce court over some custody battle telling people how my dowsing rods had predicted a break-up. I thought I had better stick to ghost hunting or looking for spirits, and asking questions from the Other Side.

Many times checking the backgrounds and doing history checks on the houses investigated have often helped us figure out what spirits might be there or who had died in the house.

This allows us to ask certain questions with the dowsing rods or leads us to specific places within the home. Sometimes history checks have helped to prove that our clients' evidence was true. Also questions answered when doing EVP sessions have helped to clarify important points in addition to the dowsing rods. EVP stands for "electronic voice phenomenon." When I ask a question of the dowsing rods, I cannot hear what is being said in response with my own ears so in addition to the response using the rods, the digital recording may pick up voices otherwise unheard.

This is me dowsing a very old mental asylum, also known as a Poor House. My dowsing rods took me to the top of these stairs. When I got to the top of the stairs I actually felt something tug on my left ear very hard. I quickly looked back and there was no one near me when I felt my ear pulled. Later that night we also videotaped a black shadowy person walking down the hallway. It was on the wall to my left side. So I usually trust where my dowsing rods take me and it helps while setting up my video equipment. This asylum was so active while the Ghost Hunters of the Finger Lakes were investigating that we heard what sounded like kids running up and down the stairs.

Later on that night in the building next to this one we actually saw our first sighting of an apparition. Not one but three small little gray shadows walked directly in front all three of us. It was just out of the camera angle but the camera caught all three of our heads turning and saying, "Wow! Did you see that?" at the same time. I remembered thinking, "did I just see that?" and trying to rationalize the small gray figures in my mind. It helped that the other team members saw the same exact figures walking by us so I knew it was not just in my mind! I also had a motion light set up in front of us but pointing away from us. I asked for a direct response from any spirit there, and the motion light instantly came on. This I was able to catch on video. We also found the mental asylum area where the jail cells were still standing. I stood inside the cell and I have to say it felt very creepy there. The front of the cell had a small door in it where it looked like they slid food through. Just looking at that I knew the patients were not treated very well there. It must of have been torture staying in that cell and having food slid through the door with little or no human contact. While doing some research I later found out that there were hundreds of deaths in this Poor House, many suicides and some murders that left behind high amounts of energy.

SUICIDES

Please note: death by suicide is extremely sensitive and can be triggering. If you have thoughts of suicide or are worried that someone is thinking of taking their life, there are resources available. The Suicide Hotline can be reached 24/7 at 1-800-273-8255.

While dowsing and letting people ask "yes" and "no" questions for the spirits to answer them, it seemed to help the family and gave them some closure, especially with suicides and the grief families were feeling after a family member had taken his or her own life. I could also see the guilt and negative feelings they were feeling while speaking through the dowsing rods. Their guilt would seem to lift when they received answers which gave them some much needed peace. Most of the time, the activity in the house would calm down after dowsing. It almost seemed that the spirits were also at peace too after getting some communication to the owner or family member.

Almost all of the suicide victims would say through the dowsing rods that it was not their family's fault and asked them not to blame themselves because those who had died owned their actions for taking their own lives. Another message that was usually expressed was that the deceased were okay but some were still dealing with what they had done in their previous lives as a result of cutting their last lives short.

One message which would stick with me was on one of the EVPs that I had gotten during a suicide case. I asked while doing an EVP session if there was any information that the suicide victim wanted to tell his sister. A clear but faint man's voice said, "I'm here with Bob."

I was not sure what this meant as no one had mentioned a Bob to me. When I sat down with the sister and went over the evidence from the investigation, I mentioned that I had gotten a strange EVP when I asked her brother to give me a message for her, and I got a man's response back that said, "I'm here with Bob."

The lady started to get very emotional and started crying .I could not figure out why she was acting this way. I asked, "Is this connected somehow to your brother?"

She quickly said, "Yes! My brother's best friend in college was a man named Bob! He died in a tragic motorcycle accident about six months after my brother had passed away."

I thought that was a huge message from her brother. That would be who he was hanging out with on the Other Side if he could. They were great friends in college and it would make sense. Another thing she said was that the voice that came through in the EVP sounded just like her brother. You could tell she was relieved to know her brother was okay and hanging out with his best friend on the other side.

I was quite impressed with the evidence we collected. We actually seemed to be helping grieving people who were suffering from loss after the tragic deaths of their loved ones. When I first started out investigating haunted places it was more to get evidence or encounter spirits but with the suicide cases and seeing how we were helping people, my primary goal became more to help families find peace and gain some sense of closure after a tragic loss of their family members. It now was not so much to find spirits for the thrill of it. Usually most of the family members wanted to know, "What if we could have stopped our loved one from taking his or her life? Could we have intervened in some way to prevent the suicide?"

Most of the responses from the victims while dowsing were that it was not anyone's fault. Most of the suicide victims had taken blame for their own actions and did not blame others for what they did. Many of the family members usually felt they should have done more at the time, so this allows for people to have closure and ease their guilt. I feel for anyone that has had someone die from a suicide. There is usually a lot of grief and anger left over and many times I do think this is the cause of activity after a suicide. After all strong emotions can stir or cause activity in a home. It can be hard to let go of family members that have died from suicide. Some times with strong religious views of families they think their loved ones may be in hell or haven't crossed due to the suicide act being a sin. While dowsing or talking with mediums I have never had them say the suicide victims were in Hell from taking their own life. From what some mediums have told me they have to go through a life review and see how they could have done things in a different manner. There is no judgment on the other side only healing and resolving one's decisions while they lived. It almost seems the family members needed to hear from their love ones more and the spirits stayed around to try to communicate to them in any way they could just to let the know they were okay and try to give them some peace they needed.

Another similar case we worked on involved a young girl who seemed to be depressed for much of her life. She was beautiful and very artistic. Then one night, she decided to take her own life. I could tell that the family loved her very much and still held onto her because they did not want to let her go. I could totally understand, as the family felt the grief of losing her. The family members wanted to ask me questions about how she was doing on the Other Side. Was she okay? Did she cross over? They wanted to let her know how they were feeling also. The family members were still holding on to a lot of anger and regret. You could still feel not only energy from what it felt from the spirit there but the intense feelings the family were feeling too. I knew right away the family needed closure but also the spirit girl that took her life needed to let them know that she was okay too.

I asked what area of the house was best to speak to her while dowsing. My dowsing rods led me out to the kitchen where they crossed over a chair in the kitchen. Usually when my dowsing rods cross it's for a yes question but it also tells me where the energy is the strongest. I thought it was odd because her energy would more likely have been stronger in her bedroom or living room. While asking questions with my digital recorder going, I not only received answers from my dowsing rods, but a girl's voice was caught on my digital recorder. The same questions were answered not only by my dowsing rods, but by the spirit girl too. She seemed to be answering our questions in her own voice. It was great evidence, and it seemed to ease the family's fears and pain. One of the questions they asked was, "Was that you I saw standing by the counter last week?" A young girl's voice answered, "Yes!" The mom said, "I knew that was her and I was not imagining it!" After going through the evidence--having motion lights go off and getting a spirit girl's voice answering our questions--I was thrilled to share the evidence with the family. The mom showed me a picture of her showing where she spent much of her time while growing up. I could not believe where the photo was taken: the exact spot which my dowsing rods led me to in the kitchen and the same chair in which she was doing her arts and crafts.

The mom said she loved doing her arts and crafts and always sat in that chair on the left while doing them. The motion light on the right was being set-off by something we could not see. We were also getting very high energy spikes there.

"Okay," I said. "That makes more sense now and that is where the girl's energy was the strongest!"

I felt good after helping the family out and hoped that I gave them the peace they much needed. The next week the family had a huge clue that the girl was probably okay. The mother was taking a shower and noticed a strong feeling of something watching her. She thought it was a different feeling than before and not scary or intense in any way, but a calming energy. When she finished her shower and she started to open the shower door, but before she could, she noticed something was written on the shower door that had fogged over. She even knew whose handwriting it was by looking at the door. It was in her daughter's handwriting, and it was her daughter's name written on the shower door! I believe it was the daughter giving reassure which was much needed for this mom, and I think she got some closure from this. She sent the photo to me and it clearly shows her daughter's name written on the shower door. I was shocked but I also knew it was a great message from the Other Side and it added a healing aspect to it.

I had a lot of calls about another area, which not only had paranormal activity, but also spirits which were sensed and seen. Sometimes, the owners had only begun to see spirits while at other times, some had seen spirits all of their lives, but seemed frightened of them. Knowing from what my grandmother told me about how she could see ghosts/spirits, I figured that most of these people who had called me must have been gifted or sensitive.

CHILDREN'S SEMINAR

The Ghost Hunters of the Finger Lakes started doing seminars and telling people about our ghost stories. We did one seminar with a 5th grade class. The students were very young and we did not want to scare any of them, so we were very nervous. I was shocked to see how well-behaved they were and how quiet the school auditorium was. We asked if they had any questions or wanted to see how any of the equipment worked or was used. One question asked was, "Can your dowsing rods point to a boy named 'Reed' in this class?"

I never thought it was possible but my dowsing rods instantly pointed to a boy in the far right of the class. I walked toward the boy and asked my rods if this was the boy named "Reed." The rods quickly crossed for a "yes!" All the kids quickly said, "Wow! The dowsing rods were right!"

So I confirmed the boy's name by asking him if his name was "Reed." He looked shocked and both of his eyes opened wide. The boy said, "Yes," in a very nervous low voice. The kids seemed to be enjoying themselves and we were also learning things from them.

Later the kids would tell us many of their own ghost stories. One girl asked if animal spirits can be around us. I said, "Yes we have caught evidence of ghost pets too."

"Well," she said, "I had a small puppy and loved it very much. It was a very hyper puppy and he used to run circles around my bed with a small red ball in his mouth. He loved that red ball" she said. "One day my puppy ran out into the road and was hit by a car and killed. I had left the front gate open and the puppy ran through the gate opening and into the road. I felt so bad and guilty about it." she said. "About a month later I heard a noise by my bed. I looked down and could see the red ball moving around. It scared me at first. All of a sudden the ball started to rise up off the ground in the air and started floating around my bed in the same circles, like my puppy used to do. I could not believe what was happening. Suddenly the ball stopped moving, and it just laid there on my floor. But I just knew it was my puppy letting me know he was alright and was still around me." She asked, "Do you think it was my puppy?"

"Yes, I do, and it sounds like he was just letting you know he was okay and he is still around you in spirit."

"I knew it!" she said with a beaming smile and tears running down her cheek. "Thank you. I always wondered about that, she said. The little girl seemed to be getting some closure from our little talk. Because we could see her smiling afterwards, it made me feel better to be able to talk with her about it.

I believe the guilt the little girl felt due to leaving the gate open and the little puppy being hit by the car left a huge amount of energy of feelings that needed to resolved. I think her puppy was trying to tell her he was okay and not to worry about him. You could see a happy expression on the girl's face and I believed she let go of the guilt now knowing her puppy was okay and happy and still playing with his favorite ball.

We were thankful that we did the seminar. The kids had many stories to tell us that day, and we had a great time listening to them and helping them with their questions using the dowsing rods.

DOPPELGANGERS

A doppelganger happens when someone sees a spirit or a person who appears to look like him or her. Sometimes she or he sees the same person in two different locations at the same time. This same lady claimed to be gifted after having a near death experience. One gifted woman told me a story that relates to the doppelganger-type activity. She told me this happened to her while she was in college:

One day, her boyfriend had stopped over to her house, and they started watching TV. Her boyfriend remembered he had to stop by his place and pick something up, but he said he would be right back. The woman said, "Okay. I will see you a little bit later."

A few minutes later, there was a knock on her door and she saw her boyfriend standing in her living room. She asked him why he had returned back so soon. Had he forgotten something? Her boyfriend didn't say anything to her and he just stood there staring at her. She got extremely nervous and said, "Who are you? She realized that something was wrong and that he was not her boyfriend standing there in her living room. She yelled, "Get the hell out of here! You're not my boyfriend and I don't want you here, get out!"

Right after she screamed at him, the man dropped down to the floor to his hands and knees and scuttled backwards out of her living room and out her front door. The lady was totally freaked out, so she called her boyfriend on the phone right away and asked where he was. Her boyfriend answered the phone and said, "I'm at my house right now. I had to do a couple of things before leaving here. Why?"

Because she did not want to tell him about what had happened, she asked him just to get back to the house as fast as possible.

You could tell this experience really freaked this lady out as she was telling me this story. She knew her boyfriend lived at least 30 minutes away, and whatever this entity was seemed to be imitating him. She believed it was something menacing and evil. Entities can change their appearance and appear to people in different forms. Some call them shape shifters. I always keep this in mind when working on cases because some entities can shape shift and you never really know what you are dealing with. Family members might be seeing a little girl form when really it is something evil lurking there and just trying to gain trust or communication with the family members. Never drop your guard while investigating the paranormal. It can get dangerous if you do.

NEAR DEATH EXPERIENCES

Other cases I investigated seemed to be connected to Near Death Experiences (NDEs). The people involved in these cases had been in accidents and died. They flat-lined and had to be brought back to life. The people who were revived would often say that they felt very peaceful when they crossed over to the other side. Some said that they wanted to stay there because it did feel so peaceful. However, it was not their time to go and they knew they had to return back to their bodies. They would wake up in the hospital with a new feeling of wakefulness. They felt things they hadn't felt before. They started seeing spirits and having paranormal or unexplained events happen around them which they could not explain. These people seemed to know things and experience more unusual activity around them. Some of them could see spirits with more frequency and accuracy than before their NDEs. Sometimes they were frightened because of their new awareness and the experiences which resulted from this new state of being. Some just accepted their new gift and were not afraid of being more sensitive. I know not all people experienced the same thing and some say they felt as they did before they died and nothing really changed, however they did not seem to be afraid of dying because they had already experience it.

When we investigate houses, I usually ask my clients if they have ever had a near death experience because sometimes it can be the owners who draw spirit activity to their homes rather than objects, locations, or the houses themselves. Some clients say, "It runs in our family," and that the grandmother or family member, was gifted so their psychic gift was inherited. The current generation received the same gift from their grandparents or parents and used that gift to become psychic mediums professionally, or to help friends and relatives. Some of them however, did not realize what was happening to them and it scared the Hell out of them!

Sometimes it skips generations so it is not passed directly to them, but a great aunt or grandmother who was gifted still passed the genes on to them. It is similar to being a gifted athlete, singer, or musician. Religious or spiritual beliefs did not seem to matter with people I have met that were gifted. People received these gifts regardless of what their beliefs were.

THE GIFTED WOMAN

One lady who could see spirits was a strict Roman Catholic and even said, "We are not supposed to believe in this stuff." She seemed frightened more than anyone I have seen. Another inexperienced ghost hunter group had told her that if she was seeing shadow people they must have been demons hunting her down and she should be very afraid of them. This was not good as this poor lady was frightened out of her mind.

When we settled on a night to go to her house and investigate, she called me at the last minute. She hesitated and then said, "Well, my dog just had puppies and I don't want to disturb her and her pups." So we settled on another night. It seemed as if she was too frightened to let us into her house to investigate. I told my sister about the lady cancelling on the investigation, but I kept thinking she would call back and change her mind about it. I got out my dowsing rods and asked them if she would call back. I received a "yes" answer. "Is she going to call me back today and say it's okay to investigate?" The rods swung in for a "yes" answer.

Probably less than an hour later, the lady called me back and said, "I changed my mind. I want to find out what is going on here, so can you come out to investigate tonight"

I told her, "No problem," as I could tell she was very nervous on the phone. We've actually had this happen more than once: People would back-out on investigations the last minute or suddenly change their minds and want us to investigate. So, we packed my car up with our equipment and headed out to the lady's house.

When we got to her home, she was on her front porch, smoking a cigarette. Her hands were shaking and I could tell she was very anxious. With our cameras rolling, I started to do some dowsing. The energy from the rods seemed to point toward the lady that was very nervous. It seemed the spirit was connected to this lady somehow. Most people who are sensitive seem to draw in the activity, which can be connected to them.

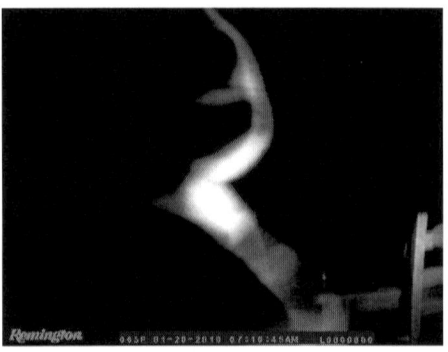

Later on in the night, we caught some good evidence: strange tapping noises and a photo of a very bright light next to the lady. The initial photo seemed to be of a swirling energy starting to form.

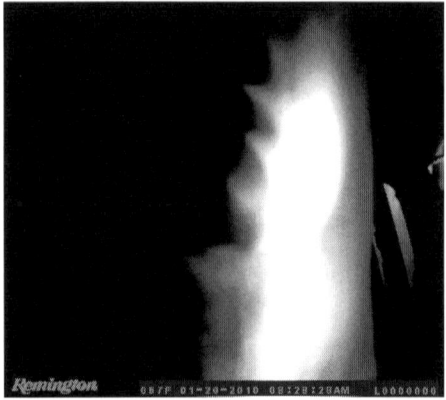

This is the second photo that was captured almost one hour after the swirling mist photo was taken. The lighted figure appeared right next to the owner. There was no flash used in this photo, only infrared lights, and all of the lights were off in the house, so there should be no visible light there.

While dowsing her home, my dowsing rods started swaying very quickly back and forth which is usually a younger child energy because it can be seen as playful or uninhibited. As I got the child energy my dowsing rods instantly pointed to the lady. I asked her if she may have lost a child or knew of a child that may have passed on. The lady started shaking and crying uncontrollably, as I seemed to hit a nerve by mentioning this. She confessed to losing a child many years back. She did not think it was her child as she lost her baby early in her pregnancy. Afterwards, it made sense to her, and she told us she could hear a child playing in/with her son's toys late at night while no one was there.

While asking questions, my dowsing rods also told her not to fear it as the spirit was connected to her. You could see her calm down, and she was happy it was not evil in any way. She then confessed to the story that the other ghost hunter group had told her. The group had said, "It must be evil," because she, "had seen black shadows," in her house. She also believed it was evil, due to the strict beliefs she held. That's why she was so frightened. I believe by her being extremely nervous and scared that she also manifested even more activity in her home. This is usually from the intense emotions stirred up by what the other ghost hunters told her. From experience I have seen this many times before and it is unfortunate that this happens. I believe when dealing with people it is always better to keep a calm presence and not jump to conclusions until you gather all your evidence. The best way is to inform the owners what may be going on in their home and try to come up with a rational explanation or inform them to what spirits may be there in their home with them.

The lady called me back a week later and told me she had heard noises coming from her son's toy area again. The next thing she witnessed was a ball moving and then the ball rolled out of the toy area and into the living room on its own. The ball even changed direction and rolled around a corner which is impossible for this to happen. She could not believe what had just happened. She was not scared of the activity and it soon calmed down, so she did not fear it anymore because she knew it was connected to her in spirit and it was not harmful in any way.

Later on this same lady became more open to the spirit world; she would not only see spirits, but interact and receive messages from the spirits. Before we met her she had always blocked her gift, though because she always thought it was something evil. We helped her get over her fear of spirits and she began letting her intuition come through. The lady later confessed that her dog never had puppies. Because she was too afraid to let us in to investigate, she had made up the story about her dog having puppies due to her being afraid of what might happen if she let us investigate there. I am glad she changed her mind because it helped her overcome her fears and changed her whole outlook of spirits and the paranormal.

This was one of the better cases as we not only helped the owner get over her fear of the spirit activity, but she was able to move on by helping other people through her gift of sight. I think these things do not happen by accident and that there is a purpose for meeting and helping certain people. I believe we all have a purpose in this life and are all connected in some ways.

DEER HUNTER'S GHOST

I got a call from a very concerned person about something he had experienced:

"My son was out hunting this past Saturday and he had something very strange happen to him. I was waiting for him to come out of the woods as it started to get dark out.

I heard my son yelling, 'Dad, you need to check this out!'

"'What are you talking about?' I asked my son. Then, I heard a young girl screaming in the woods nearby."

"What? A young girl? Was she hurt?" I asked.

"I don't know. All I know is that I heard her screaming in the woods over there," the man on the phone said. He continued, "So, we headed over where we heard the screams and found out there was a very old abandoned home there. We did not know the house was there until we checked out where the screaming was coming from. As I got closer to the house, I got a cold chill that shot through my spine. I actually could not move and felt paralyzed there in the spot I was standing. I cannot explain what it felt like, although it felt like an energy buzzing through me.

My wife walked over and felt it, too. My wife thought she'd seen someone in the upstairs window in the old house. 'It looked like a girl or woman staring at me,' she said."

He took a deep breath and then continued, "We were all

pretty freaked out. We looked around, but never found anyone there. We got the hell out of there because the energy was so strong and we did not want to stay there any longer."

The incident happened way out on an old, backwoods, dirt road in the middle of nowhere. I started to walk into the woods where they told me the house was located. About half-way there, I started to see the very old-looking house. I walked a little closer and realized that I had begun to feel a little light-headed. Then all of a sudden, I felt a very strong energy shoot through me. The hair on my arms shot straight up. I was actually by myself, so I was a little nervous, but I continued on anyway because I wanted to see what was making me feel this way. The house was really creepy, and I got an angry feeling from whatever was there with me. It was clear from the energy that whatever or whoever was present did not want me around.

I started dowsing to see who was there with me. I got an older man and thought that he was the one whom the angry feeling was coming from. I also got a little girl around eight years-old there. I asked the dowsing rods where the little girl was located. They took me to the back of the house, near some bushes. I took a few pictures there. Later, I noticed that there was some energy in the trees, which had appeared in the photos, but which couldn't be seen at the time the photos were taken.

If you look at the upper middle of this photo, you should be able to see the energy. There was no fog or any other mist, smog, or smoke that showed up in any of my photos. This is the spot my dowsing rods led me to. I walked to the house and went inside. I felt energy there as well, so I snapped some more photos.

If you look at the window area, you can see a strange mist going out the window. There were no other cameras or equipment there. I could not explain the weird mist as it seemed to be leaving the room I was in.

Actually, the energy did not feel as bad as it was during the daytime, which was weird. I got some very high EMFs in the window area, which was also weird because there was no electricity at all in the house. Later on, I found out an older man had hung himself there. I did not know it when I was dowsing, but it may have been the older male I received information about with the dowsing rods.

The girl is still a mystery, though. Another medium told me a little girl was murdered by an older male there. I do not know if that is true, but maybe it ties into the male that took his life there. I know my dowsing rods took me out back where the little girl was, so maybe she is buried in the backyard. Investigations do not usually tell the whole story, but the evidence of high EMFs and EVPs from an older male and a young girl there in the house tells some of the story.

One night, I went back to this old house and heard a shuffling sound right behind me while I was alone upstairs. I actually caught the noise and my motion light going on and off several times on my video recorder.

The last two photos I took were up at the window area. Can you see what looks like a figure standing in each of the windows?

GHOSTS ARE REAL

THE HAUNTED COLLEGE STUDENT

Another person in the local area had contacted me. He was a grad student at one of the nearby colleges. He had recently experienced a lot of death and loss. Within the last few years, a close friend of his had taken his own life and some family members close to him had passed away. Not surprisingly, he had a lot of ghostly activity in his apartment. He was very frightened at the time, though because of what he had seen. The activity seemed to get worse every day.

One day, he witnessed speaker wires floating over by his computer. He watched as the wires free-floated for at least ten seconds and then dropped to the ground like someone had been holding them in their hands and just let go of them. He could also hear his computer flash on and off and the computer keys push down as if someone was typing on his computer. He could hear people walking around his apartment at night, often bumping into things. One night, he heard footsteps walking down the hallway next to his room. He looked up and saw a woman walking close by his bedroom door and then into the bathroom. The bathroom door then closed! A few minutes later, the toilet flushed. He called out, thinking it was his mother, "Mom, are you alright? It's three o'clock in the morning. What are you doing up this late?"(NOTE: Some people think 3am is the witching hour and activity seems to hype up at this time for this reason. You may notice that a lot of activity happens in the middle of the night for this reason.)

No one answered him, so he looked out his bedroom door. A minute later, his mother answered him, but her voice came from her bedroom and not the bathroom area. His mom said, "Who are you talking to? I've been in my bedroom sleeping all night."

He got up and slowly walked to the bathroom door. Something walked into the bathroom and someone or something had closed door. When he slowly opened the door and looked behind it, there was no one there. He was very frightened at that moment because he was sure that there was some kind of paranormal activity going on in his home.

He called our group very stressed out and wanted me to come over and find out what was happening there. When I arrived, I set-up my trail camera and then started asking questions to get an idea of what was happening there. He told me that people in his family were gifted and that he even sat in on séances when he was only six years of age. On the nights after the séances, he had some bad experiences with spirits which he still felt were around him.

One night, he saw a very evil-looking man with a hooded cloak on, standing by his bed. The next morning, he woke up with scratches on his arms. As you can imagine, this scared the hell out of him. He moved up here to the upstate NY area, but his place had been quiet and he had had no issues until the deaths occurred.

He also told me that he had witnessed a dark, cloud-like shadow floating over him as he lay in his bed. As the dark shadow opened up and he could see an evil face staring directly down at him. This was the same black shadow figure he had seen when he was younger. This apparition seemed to have somehow followed him here to his new place. This made me think of the séances and maybe there was an attachment to him from doing the séances. I had the feeling this was a very bad energy attached to him.

Another night, he had seen a young, child-like figure poking his head over the end of his bed at night. Then, the same spirit boy was sitting on his night stand another night. He said that he had been meditating more lately, and it seemed to make him even more sensitive because he was having more visions. He was hoping by mediating it would help him control his visions better.

While he was telling me all of this, he was clearly terrified; a sign that what he was saying was legitimately true. He was shaken by all of these experiences and as the activity increased, he began to worry that he was going crazy so he needed some answers to explain what was happening to him.

I said, "Well, let's get some photos and maybe my ghost box will provide some proof." A ghost box gives spirits a way to communicate. The box constantly runs through channels which have talker chips installed in them, so it can be manipulated by spirits to give us random, vocalized messages. I used the box for the first time on this case. It was not fully assembled because it came as a kit, so the pieces had to be soldered together. I had two college students with me at the time. They were investigating the paranormal and doing a story on my ghost group, so they witnessed what happened next.

The ghost box was very quiet until the college student's mother wanted to ask a question. She had just lost her husband, so she asked if she could say something to him. I said, "Sure go ahead and see what response we get."

She mentioned she loved him, missed him a lot, and wanted a message from her late husband. The ghost box started to make some popping sounds and then came a message from the box: "I love you! I love you!"

Next, the box said the grad student's full name. I thought, "Wow! This ghost box *does* work!" It was my first experience seeing the ghost box in action. His mother got pretty emotional hearing, "I love you!" from the ghost box, but what she was feeling was happiness. She actually started to tear up. I thought that it was great to receive a message like that from the Other Side.

The college students were also shocked and starting writing down notes very quickly with their eyes wide open. "Is that thing a recorder or something?" the college students asked.

"No, it's not. As a matter of fact, it can only put-out random words as they are pre-programmed into the speaker chip," I replied.

Their eyes grew bigger. "Really? To get a message from the Other Side and to say the name of someone here in the room with us is very good evidence."

I said, "Yes. What are the chances of that happening? Some people don't believe in the talker boxes, but I have had messages given through the box that could never be explained." We all heard the messages, and it turned a lot of non-believers into believers that night.

The next day, I started going through my photos from the trail camera. I could not believe what I had captured with the camera. An apparition of a woman! The partial lady figure seemed to be floating very high off the ground. There was also a picture of one of the college students with her, so I could compare the height of each person.

I sent the photo to the college student to let him know what I had captured that night. The students could not believe what was next to them as they both knew there was no lady in the room, especially not a lady with a dress on. The dress was very fancy. We could see her shoulders, but she didn't have a head?

There is what looks like a headless person in this photo and wearing a white dress. The shoulders of the lady are visible, but the person does not appear to have a head. There was no one physically in the room with a dress on. You decide for yourself what you see.

The man said one of his relatives always wore fancy dresses like that. It made me wonder if the apparition was connected to him. We could also hear the computer keys being clicked down like someone was typing on them. However, there was no one near the computer. One grad student mentioned that he could hear a lot of noise by his computer at night, so it is clear that something was going on.

In the upper, right-hand corner, there is a swirling, black mist floating over the home owner's head. The owner later told me it was the same black mist he witnessed floating over him that had the evil looking face in it.

That night, we also experienced the scent of freshly-cut roses in the room. The smell was strong, as if someone was waving these perfumed flowers right under our noses. We looked for air fresheners in the home, but could not find where the smell was coming from. Along with this experience, we witnessed a light in the bedroom pop and fill with black film inside, like it had received a high voltage of electricity. We also recorded some very high EMF hits on our EMF detectors.

I set up one of my trail cameras in the bedroom, shooting directly at the computer. I wanted to catch whatever was making the typing noises. After looking through my photos I realized that the camera had captured a full-body apparition standing by the computer.

A few minutes after the photo on the left was taken, I

walked into the bedroom and leaned over the desk to set my digital recorder down by the computer. The camera captured what appeared to be an apparition hovering over the computer right in front of my face.

I have received mixed feedback on this photo. Others felt that this could have been one of the people attending the investigation. However, notice how solid I seem to be in comparison with the spirit; you can actually see the blinds through the apparition. Also I am leanin down over the desk so a person would need be standing where the desk is to be shown in this picture. I will leave it up to you to decide.

We realized this grad student was very sensitive and seemed to draw spirits to him. One psychic medium said it best, "He (the grad student) is like a lighthouse: the spirits can sense that he can see and communicate with them, so they are drawn to him." After many investigations, I do think this is true. Some people seem to draw in spirits to them due to being open and sensitive to them.

There is an update to this case: We had to go back to follow up on more activity in this man's home. The man said that he received a call from a very gifted woman for the purpose of protecting his home and himself from any ghostly activity there. She said that she knew he was having trouble, that she was a gifted psychic medium, and that she could help him. The man decided to allow this woman to help him, but as a result of following this woman's advice, the paranormal activity started to increase in a frightening way. The spirits which appeared in his home seemed to be more of the demon variety than the nice, "I just walk down your hallway from time to time," type. So, he called her back up. "It's worse now. What should I do?" the man asked.

"I have a candle for you and for 700 dollars, I can fix the activity in your home if you buy the candle from me," the woman said. After that phone call, the man contacted me and asked what he should do. "She is a scam artist," I told him, "Don't do it. She is gonna rip you off."

Although the college student realized that the woman had scammed him, the paranormal activity in his home was really too much to handle. Wanting instant relief from this scary mess, he ended up buying the candle from the woman anyway. He set the candle out and burned it according to the woman's instructions. Unfortunately, the candle had been charged with negative energy or some type of bad spell which released even more chaos into his place. As you can guess, it did not fix the problem and the activity worsened and increased even more.

He called the lady back and said, "It didn't work. The activity is worse, if anything. What should I do?"

The woman said, "Well, for 9,000 dollars, I can really end all the issues in your home and rid it and you of the evil entities there."

The man realized now that this woman was truly scamming him. But, he also started to wonder just how this lady knew that he had just received a 9,000 dollar student loan grant? How could she ask for the exact amount of money that he just won from the local college? How did she know that information, as it was not public knowledge? He started to wonder if this lady was actually causing the activity in his home on purpose through whatever kind of witchcraft she may have been using on him.

That week, the activity grew worse. He started to hear growling and grunting noises by his bed at night. As you can imagine, he was scared out of his mind and he could not sleep at all. The curtains started to rise out by his bed and he could see a large pig's head shape in the curtains. This happened a few times. He also started to see a black, shadowy mist of an evil looking man sitting on his bed, staring directly at him. There were also many other spirit figures in his home. Then, one morning, he woke up to a black figure lying next to him in his bed. The black figure reached over and grabbed him and started to attack him while he was laying there.

It was at this time that I received the call to investigate this case. The college student was extremely upset as he was telling me all of the information he had left out in his previous phone conversations with me. I never heard a grown man so upset. His voice was wavering as he spoke to me. I wondered why the activity had gotten worse. Then, he told me about the lady and what he had done in more detail. He said, "I know you told me not to do it, but I was so scared that my fear got the best of me. I gave the woman 700 dollars..." and he told me what happened. Here is the more detailed version of the story:

"Well, you can't exactly say it was the woman who caused the problem until we investigate it," I told him. "Let's not jump to conclusions until we check it out."

The next day, the same man rang again, totally freaking out. He said, "There was a dark shadow person, lying next to me on my bed. I looked over and made eye contact with this thing and it reached over and grabbed my groin and started to attack me! That's not all: I have woken up with scratches on my face, but I did not tell you that yesterday. I was too afraid that it would do this as a result of contacting you guys."

"I wonder if he knows we can get rid of it, and that's why the shadow person attacked you, I said. "Well, this is an extreme case. We need to get out there and get rid of whatever is in your home," I said. "It sounds really aggressive and dangerous now." I had prepared the holy water solution and we had all of our other gear ready to go. I quickly called a psychic medium that I really trusted to get rid of something bad like this. She said, "Oh, yeah. I can help you" as she was already picking-up this poor man's attacks. "He needs our help, so let's get this done tonight!

I agreed as I don't think this guy would ever go back to sleep in his bed after what happened to him. As we were driving to the man's house, the medium said, "Oh, I'm getting a female involved in this activity. Why am I seeing this?" she said.

"Well, I think I know," I said. She continued, "This man does not like this woman, but for some reason, he called her for something and she did something to him," the medium said. Oh, man. She was right on with the information she was getting. "All I know is that she made this happen and caused the problems there," the medium said. I didn't say much, but I agreed with her and said, "You sound like you are on the right track," I said. When we arrived at the house, we could feel the extreme pressure in his home. It was unnerving, but I had felt this heavy pressure before and knew that whatever was there was causing this. When the medium walked into the home after me, it seemed to go away a little bit. All of us actually felt the whole room shift in a different direction. "Oh, whatever is here is hiding from me," she said and started to laugh.

"That's because I'm not afraid of you," she said, laughing. The man told the medium of the attacks and he looked like he had been through a war. His face was very white, pasty-looking, and overly tired. "I haven't slept in weeks," he said, barely keeping his head up. "I hope you guys can help me out."

"Yeah, I will get rid of this thing, and the entities here," the medium said. I had to laugh because this medium was so direct. She also didn't care at all if anything heard what she said. She was letting the entity know she was not afraid, and it seemed to lighten the mood, which felt very dense in the home. "It's hiding from me right now," she said. "It knows what I can do and that I can get rid of him. That's why it's hiding right now. Did you go to different countries and travel a lot?" she asked the man.

"Yes. I have traveled to foreign lands and even did a school project on ancient ruins and was involved in some digs there."

"Well, whatever attached to you followed you back here. But something other than that is here and it's because of a woman that promised to help you."

The man said, "Oh my God! She did do something to me! I knew it," he said. "This woman was doing rituals and causing a lot of this mess," the medium said. The man confessed to her about what happened and about the money he gave to her to stop it. "Yeah well, she caused this because she wanted more money from you. You have to watch out – some people use their gift for bad and this woman was doing just that. I will get rid of it," she said very casually as she always does. I have to laugh because this medium is matter-of-fact when dealing with entities and spells/rituals, etc. "Let me see where it leads me," the medium said. She walked into the man's bedroom.

"Oh, yeah. It's hiding in here," she said. I was sitting on the bed when she said, "Be careful by your foot. At that exact time, my foot went ice cold. "Whoa!" I said. "What the?!"

"It came out from under the bed and just went over your foot. It is attached to it. Just shake your foot off and move to the other side there," she said. So, I gave my foot a shake and it felt better, but it was still very cold. The medium said that when I shook my leg, she watched the entity fly through the air and go off from my foot and go into the middle of the man's back standing next to her. He let out a groan as this happened. The medium just laughed and said, "Well, let's get rid of this thing." It was like she was going to the mall for shopping; it did not faze her one bit. I sprayed some holy water on my leg as I did not want anything attached to me so I started visualizing a white light around me as a protective bubble. I had my EMF meter out and it started spiking and picking up on some huge amounts of energy in the room. "Wow!" I said, "The EMFs were extremely high, especially by the man's bed."

The medium started cleansing the house. She used many different kinds of sage, and I had my holy water with cedar. Just for an experiment, I held my EMF meter out, just in front of me, while the medium was cleansing the home. There were huge amounts of EMFs shooting through my EMF meter where I was standing. I could also feel it, but wanted to scientifically gauge it while it was happening. I have to say that one could see the medium ridding the home of the negative energy. It always amazes me when I see things like this. Later, after the medium also cleansed the man with the sage and blessed him, the man started shaking. He said that he could feel it leaving his body and at one point, it looked like he was going to pass out. "I am really dizzy," he said with his eyes rolling back into his head. His body started to fall backwards. "Holy crap! Are you all right?" I asked the man. He didn't respond right away. "Yes, I feel what was around me left and I feel better now."

"Oh, I can see the color going back into your face," I said. "Well, your face has color in it now."

"Really?"

"Yes. You were white as a ghost," I said, starting to laugh to myself for saying that.

The medium said, "Take your EMF meter and check the house now." So, I took out my EMF meter and walked through the house. "Wow! It stayed on zero the whole time," I said.

"That's because it's gone and nothing is here now." It felt so peaceful and light afterwards. "It feels so much different now." The man noticed it, too. "I can't thank you guys enough," the man said. "And it didn't cost you 9,000 dollars," the medium laughed. "We don't charge for cleansing, so I think you got the better deal here."

The man said, "I was so scared I almost paid more money to that woman."

The medium noted, "I can say that she caused most of the activity here in the first place. Most of it was her and some of it was because you are so gifted the other entities here followed you home." She continued, "The spirits were very old; from ancient places, though. But with you traveling to some very old countries and ancient places, all of that makes sense to me now. I sent the bad entities back to the woman who put the curse on the candle, so she can deal with her own mess she created." I was impressed by her ability and happy that the family could have some peace of mind.

The psychic medium also said, what you put out there can come back and bite you! In this case, it was true. The two dogs sitting on the couch looked relieved now, too."

"I know they were seeing the entities, too," the man said.

"I'm glad that's all over with," I said as we relaxed on the couch, talking. The medium knew she had to work with the man as he did not know how to protect himself and hadn't learned to deal with his gift.

"Stop by my house, and we will have to talk some more about your gift," the medium said. "You can't keep having these spirits bothering you like this." The man looked extremely relieved and happy that we helped him. I got a big "thank you" phone call the very next day. The man said that the home was so much calmer that he felt at peace now. "It was the first night in a long time I actually slept all night," he said.

Another case had resolved, and with good results in the end. I should say, "Be advised to never trust anyone who asks for large amounts of money to rid anything from your home. These people feed on the fear people are having in their home and use it to scam them. They use their gift for bad and they are out there."

PSYCHIC MEDIUMS

After meeting and speaking to many psychic mediums who tell me they do indeed have activity in their homes, I tell them that they have to cleanse their homes after doing their readings, so they can live in peace without spirits trying to bother them. Sometimes, however, they do see and have spirits come to them because they are, after all, mediums and can see and communicate with them.

One medium I met truly by accident. The lady was probably in her thirties and was a waitress in a restaurant and she walked up to me and asked me if she could tell me something. She said, "There is a man here in spirit with me and he says he knows you and is connected to you. He will not leave me alone and said he must get a message through to you."

The medium started to tell me what this man looked like and started explaining how he was connected to me. She said, "He has a hammer in his hand and he wants to build the deck bigger. He looked tired but wanted to help with the deck. I can see the house – it's an older blue house now, but it used to be a different color: white, I think. It was a farm house and it had a barn next to it. I can see chicken wire by the barn where there were chickens kept."

I told the medium, "You just told me what my grandma's old house looks like. There was a barn next to the house, but was torn down many years ago. My sister lives in the house and it is blue now. You were talking about my dad who just died less than three months ago: He wanted to help build the deck behind my grandma's old house, but at the time, he was too weak. So, he just watched and gave out suggestions. As he watched us build the deck, he said it was too small and if he were building it, he would have made it bigger. No one would have known that, except my dad and very few family members". The next thing she told me I didn't even know the answer to. The medium said, "He wants to tell you he is okay, but he also wants to prove it's him by me telling you this."

I said, "Okay?"

"Your dad says he has a grey box under his bed and he has some personal items in the box. He has an old shaver, some war medals, tags, a very old-looking pipe, and a cross."

The medium continued, "Your dad is okay. Don't worry about him; he is fine and does not feel the pain anymore." She went on to tell me that my father's arm was sore and about how he was feeling when he was sick in the hospital. My dad had a Pic Line or Broviac inserted in his arm, but it became infected and was very painful. No one outside of the family would have known that information, only a family member who was close to him would have known about it.

As the medium was giving me a reading I said, "I don't know of any grey box, but I will check it out later. Thank you so much for everything you told me. No one would have ever known that about my family."

The psychic medium was very nice and just continued on waiting on other tables working like normal. What a gift to be able to give messages from the other side! We were thrilled to have received a special message from my dad. I had been thinking about him a lot lately, and it gave me some closure I much needed at the time.

My curiosity was killing me and I had to see for myself if the box was really under my dad's bed. When I arrived at my mom's house, I told her about what had happened and what the psychic told me. "So, can I look under your bed and see if the grey box is there?" I asked.

She said, "Sure. See what you find. I'm not sure what's under there."

As I looked under her bed, I could see a box. I thought, "No way!" So, I grabbed the box lying under the bed and pulled it out. It looked like the grey, older metal box that the medium had told me about. "Holy crap!" I thought because I could not believe the psychic medium was right about the grey box. However, was the psychic right about the contents inside it? I quickly opened the grey box and looked inside. I could not believe my eyes: There was an old shaver, an old pipe, and a war metal tag inside it.

Here are the contents inside the metal box, including the cross, metal and shavers the medium told me about.

"Wow!" I said. "She was right on everything." We all looked at each other with a very amazed, "no way" expression on our faces. The medium must have been speaking to my dad. How would the psychic have known that information?

Years had passed, and I had always wondered about this psychic medium. While investigating a haunted pub, I looked down on the table and noticed a psychic medium's card there. The card belonged to the same medium; the same one who had read for me many years ago. "What a coincidence!" I thought. I called the psychic medium up and told her that I investigate haunted places as part of the Ghost Hunters of the Finger Lakes.

She said, "It was not by accident that we met. It was clearly for a reason." This medium went on to help me with many cases and help resolve some of the issues they were having there.

I met another medium psychic after reading an article on her in the local newspaper. I had contacted her mom as this psychic was only 16 years old. I thought she could possibly help me with some other local cases here. I wanted to see if she was any good at reading houses, so I asked her if she could stop by a very active house and see what she got there. I didn't include any details of the case, so she had to go in the house with no details. [This is the best way for mediums as you do not want to lead them in any wrong direction.]

I heard that was there was a young boy who refused to sleep in his bed at night. The little boy would wake-up screaming in the middle of the night. He would say he was seeing people in his room and that they were bad people and very scary-looking. I did a "walk through" of the house earlier and got some high EMFs which told me that there was some activity going on there. Again, EMF stands for "electrometric field," which in theory is said to be caused by a spirit. After we die, we still have electrical impulses and energy. EMF meters can pick up on this energy and let us know there is some form of energy around us. You have to rule-out any natural sources in a home, such as electrical outlets, bad light switches, or bad wiring which also gives out high EMF fields.

After investigating the house and getting pretty good evidence, there was something I thought the psychic medium could help out with: to read the house to see what she could find there. As always, I did not give out any details about the house to the medium; only that the kids were having a hard time with whatever was in it. When the medium arrived, she quickly picked up on the spirits there and said, "There is a little girl and boy spirit here." She pointed down the hallway and said, "I see them together, holding hands at the end of the hallway." Then the medium was quickly drawn to the boy's bedroom where the boy could not sleep at night. It was also where I got some very high EMFs. At one point while we were there, one of the little girl's toys in the closet started playing by itself. It was a push button-style toy. The door was closed when this happened. When I opened the closet door and looked at the toys, I could see that the button had been pushed down, as if someone was pushing the buttons on the toy, even though I could see no one was around it.

The little girl that lived there pointed it out to me and also said, "Yup. They like to play with my toys a lot." She seemed to be used to the spirits there and did not have a problem with them. She could see a little girl spirit in her room as the little girl spirit sat on the corner of her bed at night. "I like the little girl spirit," she said. "She is not mean at all."

The medium said, "Well, I don't think the little girl spirit will leave due to the spirit having a close relationship with her." The medium walked into the boy's bedroom. "I don't like this room's energy. It's bad in here." The medium then asked me to point my trail camera to a window in the boy's bedroom where she was picking up some negative energy. So, I quickly pointed my trail camera to where she was standing. You could tell that there was something there. She did not like it because she sensed it was a very negative energy. She said, "There is a dark energy here and it's not good. I can see a black cloud and it's above my head here, by the window." What I got was unnerving, and really proved what she was seeing: the black energy she had picked up on in the room.

You can see the psychic medium reacting to the black energy, starting to form over her head. She had started to react to the negative energy there, and you could see her getting agitated over it. The medium said, "I have to leave this room and regroup myself." She was visibly shaken by what she had felt there in the room.

Just after she left the room, I got another photo. It was exactly what she was telling me about: the dark energy had grown and darkened even more in the room. I had the photos to prove it. I was blown away by this evidence.

The photo above was taken six minutes later. It shows the black, swirling energy caught by my camera. What impressed me most about this experience was that the medium was able to tell me where the black energy was, even though it wasn't visible, and that I was able to prove what she was seeing through the photo that was taken because the camera captured the image of the dark energy.

What I like about these trail cameras is that they are time-stamped in each photo. So, there is no mix-up with the time when the photos were taken. The date and time stamps also proved that the medium was actually seeing something at the same time that it was actually present in the room.

The black mist started to form over the medium's head and right after it did so, she stepped-out of the lens frame. Then the cloud turned even darker. The psychic medium decided to perform a clearing of the negative energy. She smudged the area with special incense and said some prayers, and asked the spirit to leave. By the time she was finished doing her work, the room did feel lighter. The next thing the psychic did was mention a young man with a rooster-like haircut, but he was connected to the owner in the house. She said, "There is a man here who wants to give the owner a message. He has many different shades of colored hair and a Mohawk haircut."

I was thinking, "Okay. She has to be way off on this one."

But the owner was surprised. "Oh, my God!" she exclaimed. "I know who you're talking about. My best friend in high school was killed in a very bad car accident. I think about him all the time. I was thinking about him just the other day, actually."

"Well, he wanted to let you know he is okay now and not to worry about him. He crossed over and has no pain anymore," the medium said. She gave the owner another personal message that only she would know about. It was great to see how accurate this medium was. The boy could now sleep in his room at night. So, she was also great at clearing the room of its negative energy. This medium always seems to be on target with her reads of the houses we investigate, and she always amazes me with her accuracy.

PSYCHIC NURSE STORY

I hear many ghost stories from different people every day. It's amazing how many paranormal experiences people have in their daily lives. They want to share their experiences, but do not want to be judged in any way. So many times, they only tell people who they know are trustworthy and who are not going to laugh at them. They usually start off with, "You might think I'm crazy, but this is what happened to me. I usually say, "No, not at all. Tell me what happened to you as I'm curious to know."

One lady was a nurse and worked in a hospital for a number of years. She was also a psychic medium and could see spirits. She said, "I have many stories, but here is one that sticks with me."

"As I was doing my normal nursing tasks one day, I noticed a woman standing off to the side of me. I knew right away that she was not a person because I could see right through her. I also noticed she was wearing a nurse's outfit, like I was. As I looked closer, I recognized her. I had worked with this nurse about five years ago until she passed away. She was trying to get my attention, so she waved me over to her. As I walked closer, she started pointing down the hallway. She said, 'Go to room 301 now. It's urgent that you go there right now.'

I could tell she meant business. So, I rushed down the hall and looked into room 301. The patient who was in there was not breathing and looked pale. He needed attention right away.

I worked on him until he was breathing again. Now, I know the spirit nurse was warning me by telling me this patient needed help right away. She was still helping to save lives, even after her death. She shows up now and again to help me with the patients, and I'm happy she looks out for me."

    I thought this was a great story and will always remember it well.

PERSONAL STORIES

I have heard many personal stories about serious car accidents during which the people felt calm and knew someone was with them. One lady told me she could smell the scent of perfume as if there was someone in the car with her, just before having a bad car accident. She said, "I don't know how I survived it as I veered off the road. I closed my eyes and hoped for the best. Someone was looking out for me and seemed to be steering the car because I just missed some big concrete structures that would have killed me for sure." Somehow she walked away with only minor scratches.

Many people have told me stories of walking away from a car accident without any scratches on them when they should have died. I heard lots of stories involving the World Trade Center. They should have gone to work that day, but for some reason they did not go or did not make it to work. I've even heard stories of pets that were still around their owners, even after their deaths.

I have experienced pet ghosts myself. One night, I felt my cat jump up on my bed and start doing his usual circles on the bed until he got comfortable. I asked my wife, "Do you feel the cat walking on the bed?"

She responded, "Yes. I can feel it, too."

Finally, he stopped moving around. I could actually feel the cat lie down behind my leg, resting against it like he usually did. Well, this is usually not a problem, except that our cat had died several months ago before this and we did not have any other animals in the house at that time. We could both feel the cat walking on our bed. When I asked her to turn on the lights and we both could see, there was nothing was there on my leg. It was a strange but cool experience that I must say made me a believer in animal after life and I know animal spirits can interact with us as well after they die.

THE BAYLOR HOUSE

One of the more haunted houses I investigated would be the Baylor house. We heard so many stories about the house and how it had been extremely haunted. Attached to the house was a community center for kids. Many kids would go there and play sports like basketball. One story is that the balls would be rolling around the gym floor when no one was around. one of the children would point and say look there is a kid playing with the balls over there. But when the coach looked over at the ball he could only see a ball bouncing on its own and no child. When the coaches would lock up and turn the lights off for the night weird things would happen there. Many times the lights would turn back on by themselves and the person would have to go back into the gym and turn the lights back off. one night After locking up and getting ready to leave the person could hear a very loud slamming noise coming from the upper attic area. Thinking someone was in the house, he walked upstairs to where the slamming sounds came from. He looked around the corner and could see a door to the attic opening and closing almost like someone was opening and then slamming the door shut. Then the door would open again. He looked closer and noticed no one was there behind the door like he thought. As he turned back around the door slammed even louder. He quickly ran out of there as fast as he could. He had enough of scary stuff for one night.

Another story was with a next door neighbor that had been working on his house one day next to the Baylor house. It was only a stone's throw away from it and he had heard about the Baylor house but never experienced anything and he did not really believe in ghosts. But that would all change that day.

He had some work to be done on his house so he set the ladder up against his siding. He started climbing up the ladder and began working on repairs that needed to be done. All of a sudden he felt a quick tug on his pants. He thought someone must have wanted something so he looked down but did not see anyone. He quickly wrote it off as wind or figured something had flown off the roof and hit his leg. He began working again on his house. Again he felt a hand grab his leg but with such force it was enough to pull him off the ladder and to the ground. Again he could not see who grabbed him but whatever it was it seemed to be trying to get his attention. Well that was it for him that day as he did not go back up the ladder again. I do not blame him really as it sounded pretty scary.

There were so many stories about the house being haunted. One person said they heard disembodied voices coming from different areas of the house and some people have even seen full bodied apparitions walking around in the house. It was enough for me to want to investigate the house. We quickly found out who the owner was and asked if it was okay to investigate the empty late 1800s home. He was okay with it and told us a few more stories about some of the workers that had been working on the home and having some things happen to them. One worker said he would set down his saw or hammer and go to pick it up and it would be moved to another location. He seemed irritated by the spirits moving his tools. Another worker had a door slammed on him as he had just walked through the door. There was no wind and he knew there was no way the heavy old door should have been slamming like that. He was very startled by this and never returned to work there. This made me want to investigate this old home even more. Even hearing all these stories I wanted to get my own proof or evidence of this activity.

We decided on a night and started to set up some equipment. It seemed pretty quiet that night and we did not really have anything happen yet. I figured I would walk up the stairs and start my digital recorder and hoped I would get some voices on it. I asked, "Is there anyone here with me?" Then, my dowsing rods led me to a big room across the top of the stairs. As I entered the room I instantly got a bad headache. My head felt like it was in a vise and I began to get goose bumps on my arms. It felt very strange and I could not stay in the room any longer. Before leaving the room I set my recorder down on one of the old shelves in the room. When I exited the room my headache instantly went away and my shivers and goose bumps also subsided. It seemed whatever tension was it seemed to be in the room. I was feeling the intense emotions there and reacting to it.

My dowsing rods quickly led to me to a small room down at the end of the hallway. I asked, "Who is here? A man?" No. "A girl?" No. "A boy?" I got a big cross for a yes. "This looks like a small room for a boy." I stated. I asked some questions for the boy to answer me back. I did get a response from the spirit boy but I could not hear it in the moment. (Later at home and after reviewing my digital recorder the spirit boy had said, "Take me home." It was kind of creepy to hear the boy's response so clearly. I also wondered how lost the boy must have been too. It was kind of sad at the same time.)

We continued on the investigation going further upstairs of the home. We walked up to the older part of the very top of the house. It was a small room usually called the widow's peak room apparently named because the women would wait for the men to return home and they could see them coming from far away. While walking back from the widow's peak I noticed an animal lying in the attic area. It looked very old and decomposed. It appeared like a small dog. We were not positive of this but that's what it appeared to be. I snapped a photo of the dead animal in the attic so I could see what we found there. While going over evidence I heard some very unusual sounds on my digital recorder. The first sounds came from another investigator's digital recorder. They said, "You won't believe this but I have what sounds like a small dog barking on my digital recorder!" We both knew the house was completely empty and no one was in the house with us especially any animals. Then it clicked with me that we found the remains of a small dead dog in the attic area. (The picture is not included as it is graphic in nature.) We figured it must have gotten in through a small crack in one of the doors and then could not get back out of the house and sadly probably starved to death. It was sad to think of this happening to an animal and I thought it was sad to think of the poor thing not being able to eat or get back out of the house. It must have been the dog we found there and we were pretty excited to get an animal EVP. At that point I did not think animals would come through as voices or ever get EVPs from a dog barking. You could clearly hear a dog barking on the recorder though and it echoed in the room so we knew it was caught inside the house.

I thought I better check my digital recorder and see what I got for evidence. As I turned on the recorder the very first part was me asking if anyone wanted to tell me anything. I could hear my footsteps as I walked up the stairs to the second floor. Right after I asked the question I heard a lady yell at me, "You're an asshole!"

"What the hell was that?" I said. I still couldn't believe what I had just heard. It was the first EVP with a cursing ghost I had caught. She didn't seem to want me there in the house either!

I played it back again and sure enough the lady screams, "You're an asshole" at me! I was blown away as I knew there was no one else there with me at the time and I surely knew no one had been cursing at me. I would have said something or commented on it. So I played the digital recorder further and I started hearing the lady talking again. It sounded like the same lady that had cursed at me the first time. Then a man started yelling at the lady and they began to argue with each other! I could not believe I had gotten a full blown argument with two ghosts yelling at each other. You could hear hitting sounds and the lady screamed, Ow!"

"Holy crap this man is hitting her!" I thought.

Then the lady started cursing at the man saying, "You're an asshole!" It was actually pretty sad to hear this happening. Were these spirits reenacting an event that happened a time long ago in this home? If so were they stuck here? Or just trying to show me what happened here in the house? It was pretty unnerving to hear.

I also started to remember the awful headache I had at the room right after going up the stairs. Was I feeling the argument happening at the time this was all going on? My intense headache and the hairs rising up on my arms had to be from this intense argument. Then it struck me. Could the man actually have killed the lady and I somehow recorded this event? I could clearly hear the man hitting the lady many times and then a loud thud at the end of the argument like something bad happened to her. We never ran into this before so we needed help in solving this one. I knew I had to get some answers about my evidence and try to put some pieces together. Then it hit me that maybe a psychic medium could tell us what happened there. I made some phone calls and set up a time to meet a psychic and go to the old house and see what she would say about it. I knew I could not tell her anything before we walked through the house. I wanted the psychic medium to get all of the information about the house on her own.

When the psychic arrived at the house she pointed at the front lawn. "There is a spirit on the front lawn area. They knew I would be coming and they are waiting for me." she said. When she walked through the front door she looked down and said, "There is a small spirit dog here. The dog just walked into the room over there." I instantly started thinking of the EVP of the little dog barking in the house that we had gotten on our digital recorder. I was getting excited as it seemed to all be coming together. The psychic started to walk up the long stairway to the second floor. I could tell she was getting information but not saying anything yet.

When she reached the top of the stairs she looked at me and said, "I think someone may have been killed here on the stairway. A man was arguing with a woman and he got really mad and threw the woman over this rail and down those stairs." I instantly thought about the argument of the man and woman I had gotten on my digital recorder. "Oh I just heard the whole story about this man and why he did this." the psychic said. "The lady was having an affair with another man across the road and she was sneaking back up the stairs when the man caught her. They started to argue and the rage from this man is intense! He flung this poor woman over the rail and down the stairs. I also got a man in a robe up in the attic area and he was a preacher. He did some bad things though and never crossed over. He doesn't want to be judged or might be worried where he might go if he does leave here."

"What bad things?" I asked.

"I think he molested kids when he was alive." she said.

"Oh wow that's awful." I thought, "But it makes sense he might stay here if he is going to be judged on the other side."

She continued, "There is a little boy here too and lived here at one time."

Another EVP I had gotten in a small boy's voice said, "Take me home." All my EVPs were making sense now and seemed to be connecting with my evidence that I had gotten there. During our walk through with the psychic I had noticed my motion lights were being tripped by something in the house. No one was by the motion light when I saw it flick on so I was sure it was something else there with us at the time. I had a motion camera on one of the motion lights and I was eager to go home and check it out. This is what I captured on the motion camera.

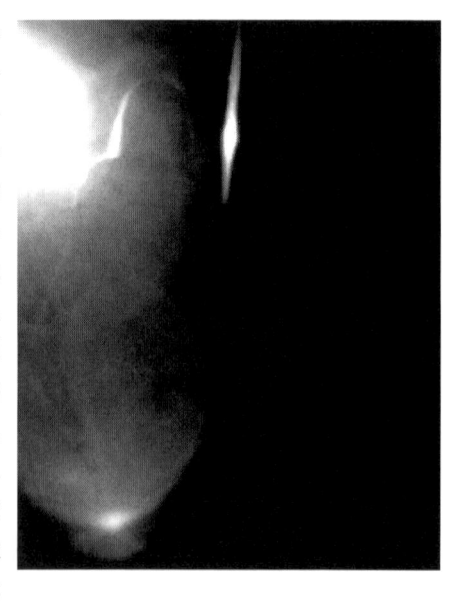

You can see at the bottom of the next photo, my motion light was going off and reflecting on a full bodied apparition. It is hard to make out the face as it is very much distorted. To me it looked like a girl because of the longer hair. Also in the photo to the right I can see a bright light like I have gotten in several of my photos. It is almost like a portal of light. In the back there was a mirror and the flash from the motion camera is reflecting back, but it also helped light up the figure in the hall way. I will let you form your own opinion about this photo. Over the years investigating this house I have gotten other photos from the Baylor house I could not explain.

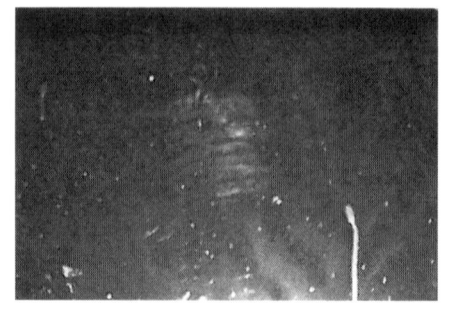

This photo was taken in the Baylor House on one of my investigations. This was in one of the mirrors downstairs in the living room area. I was shocked to see it in the mirror when I went back over my photos. Some have described it as a skull with teeth, 2 eye sockets, and an eyeball hanging from the socket on the right. Others felt it was alien or inhuman. I am still not sure what to think of this photo so I will just let you decide what it might be.

GHOSTS ARE REAL

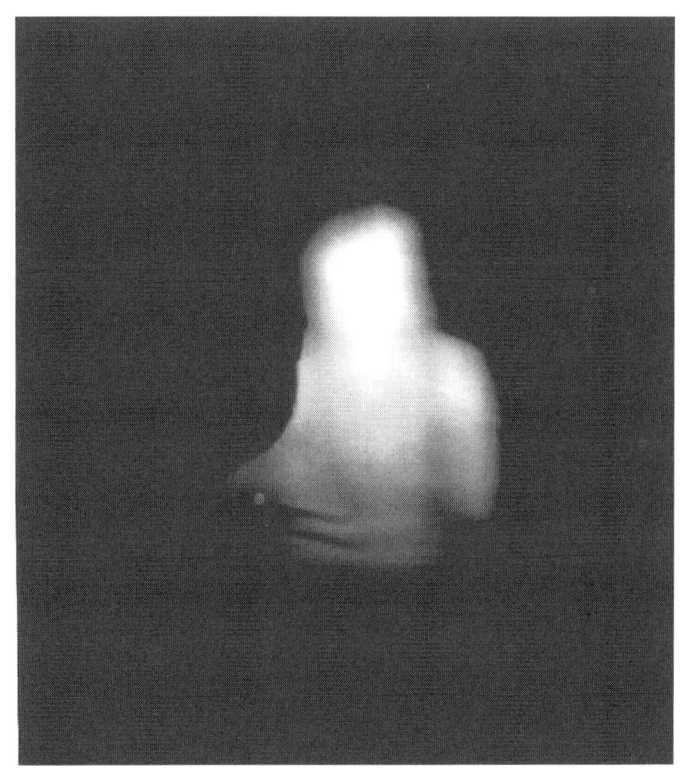

This is the psychic medium doing a walkthrough of the house. I snapped a photo of her. This is what showed up looking like on my camera. It seems whatever energy around her affected the photo. This psychic medium was later taken over by some negative entity and had to leave the house immediately. She later told me a negative spirit jumped into her and took over her. I now wonder if this photo showed the negative energy around her at the time of this photo and the spirit was getting ready to take her over as she channeled it. When I say a spirit jumped into her, I mean also like being possessed. In this case, this medium was so open to the spirits that it was pretty easy for the negative entity to take over her body.

THE MURDER/ SUICIDE CASE

This is a true story. I have chosen not to use the names of the people involved and will not disclose all of the details in this case. When we write about our investigations, we do not include confidential information such as the family's names, places or private information to protect their identities.

We were contacted by a friend who knew a family who needed help to resolve an ongoing issue in their home. They had a lot of poltergeist-type activity going on and they needed some answers to what was causing it. When I say poltergeist activity, it is usually things being mover or manipulated. It usually takes a lot of energy to move objects so you need to be careful investigating places like this.

We agreed on a time to meet with the family about the case. When we arrived, I started asking questions so we could figure out what was causing the activity in the home. The dad [I will call him, Martin] asked me, "Do you believe in the black arts?"

I thought that was a strange question, so I asked, "What do you mean by that?"

He said, "I knew a woman who said she was a white witch, and she would show me stuff that I could not explain." The man thought this woman was messing with him and possibly causing this activity. I did know some practicing pagans and people who were gifted, so this thought did not shock me at all.

"Well, I think it might be connected to the activity going on here in my home. I'm not sure, though," he said.

I have seen people who practice black magic and they've had some bad energy attached to them. So, I asked, "Were there any relatives that might have passed recently, or other deaths?"

Martin hesitated, but said, "Yes. Matter of fact, I lost my ex-wife to a brutal murder three years ago. The man who killed her took his own life by committing suicide."

From what I have seen from working suicide and murder cases, these traumatic events often leave imprints and many unanswered questions about why the deceased left this world in such an unnatural way. I was still somewhat skeptical about the murder and suicide story. I would have to research this and find some possible leads or connections to this family. He told me the name of the man involved in the murder along with more details about it. Sure enough, while researching the case, everything he told me was accurate so I started to think that the paranormal activity was possibly connected to the family somehow.

The next step was to ask what kind of activity was happening in the house to help us determine when we needed to set up our equipment. One thing that Martin told me was that the family had moved from another state. The activity had started there, but the family was having even more activity in the new location. Martin told us the following story:

"In my old house I would see black shadows. One night I watched for several minutes as a dark mist drifted over by the TV. I immediately turned the TV off as I thought it may have shorted out and was ready to catch on fire, but then a black mist moved away from the TV and came very close to me. The black mist then started forming into a person right in front of me. It stayed there for several minutes and then vanished very quickly. I also had something attack me one night that left bruises on my body. I woke up on the floor, curled up in a fetal position. I don't remember what happened. It was almost like a dream, but when I woke up, I was on the floor and I had bruises all over me. That was in our old house. We moved up to NY after that. Recently, the activity has gotten worse. One of my daughters showed me her hamster cage. I heard something moving right next to my bed. Then all of a sudden something picked this cage up and threw it across my room onto the ground. She was pretty upset to see this happen right next to her while she lay in her bed."

I started looking at the cage. There was a very big Bible lying on top of it. I asked if the Bible had been there at the time it was thrown on the floor.

"Yes, the Bible was on top of the cage and we do not have any other animals here in the house. It could not have tipped over on its own, due to the weight of the Bible on top of it. After the cage was thrown on the floor, my hamsters escaped and I've never found them," she said.

I checked the cage out: It was heavy, and after some investigation, I also decided that there was no way it could have tipped over on its own, especially with the Bible lying on top of it. We walked out to the kitchen and Martin showed me the stove that he and his wife had watched a pot of hot water move around on top of by itself. This can happen if there is water trapped between the bottom of the pot and the stove depending on the type of cook top, however I could not debunk the other odd activity. "That's not all," he said. "Many times, we will see the cabinet doors open by themselves. We find the cabinet doors open in the kitchen all the time. We have had spoons fly into the sink from the counter here.

We walked out to the living room. He pointed to the shelf area. "This container flew off the shelf and onto the floor over here. When I come home from work, I find that it has been moved around. It will be lying in the middle of the floor and strange places like that."

I thought the container had an interesting look to it. "Does this belong to anyone special?" I asked.

"Yes. That container has my wife's ashes in it," he said.

More red flags shot up. I thought that maybe it was his wife who could have been trying to send a message to her family.

"We also hear someone walking down the hallway late at night. All the family members heard the footsteps."

"What kind of footsteps? Like boots?" I asked.

"No, more like high heels, women walking in high heels," he said.

"Did your wife wear high heels a lot?" I asked.

"Yes, matter of fact, she did often wear high heels."

I thought we were on to something now. While I was talking to his younger daughter, she mentioned in a low voice that someone or something had been pulling her blankets off of her at night. "When I'm sleeping late at night, my blankets start to slide off me," she said. "When it happened, I felt like someone was there, but I didn't see anyone. This happened again to me but this time I decided to hold my blankets tight in my hand when my blankets were being pulled off me. My hands started to get pulled down along with blankets, too," she said. "Whatever it was it was really strong because I could not hold onto the blanket and finally let go." She continued, "The blankets also went very tight around me in bed and seemed to be holding me down." Her eyes were wide open. "It was scary when that happened to me. I did not want to tell my dad because I did not want to worry him," she said.

I was thinking, "Wow! This family has some type of haunting going on here." However, we needed some actual evidence to back up all of the family's claims. While talking to Martin I began to feel some type of presence near me. My arm hairs stood on end; a feeling I know well because it can indicate a spirit presence is around me. I asked if we could do a quick EVP session in the living room. He said, "Sure. Go ahead and see what you get."

Everyone else had left the house at that time. Only our ghost hunting group and Martin were present in the house, so it was very quiet. We asked several questions. It was a quick session: maybe ten questions and answers long. I had my digital recorder going when we asked the questions about the activity in the house.

We decided on a time to come back and investigate. We would bring all of our equipment with us at that time.

Later, I went over the EVPs from our quick session and was very surprised! Between the walk through and the EVP session, I'd already found not one or two, but ten EVPs! A woman seemed to be speaking to us through my recorder. The female spirit seemed to be answering some of our questions. So, we went back and set up our equipment, covering the house with video. I put a ball in the hallway and asked if someone could move it for us. Earlier, I'd also set up a grid light with many dots to catch anything that might move across the hallway area. The theory with the grid lights is that something we cannot see with our eyes might be caught moving though the lights.

I started dowsing the house and picked up energy right away. The dowsing rods started pointing to the family members like they were connected to them. I asked if the spirits were trying to communicate with them. The dowsing rods quickly crossed for "yes." I asked if the spirit of the mother was with us. Another yes. I asked about the woman who practiced the dark arts and if she was near. I received a big "no" for that question. I was picking up on an angry, frustrated feeling while dowsing. I wondered if those were the feelings from the man who committed suicide.

With my dowsing rods I asked if the guy who committed suicide was there. The rods were picking up on his energy but nothing was happening. He seemed to be there, but did not want to answer me. Maybe his feelings were the angry ones I was sensing.

My dowsing rods also told me he and she had been responsible for moving and throwing things in the house. Martin also told me of something that just happened the night before we came back to investigate. "Do you see that candle that's up in the candleholder there? While I was sitting on the couch, that candle came out of the holder and flew past my head. It was almost like they threw the candle at my head. The candle has a crack in it. Just take a look at it."

I checked the candle and it was broken in the center, although it was sitting pretty tightly in the candle holder. "It would take a lot of energy to do that," I said.

"Yes," Martin said nervously, "I know."

As we waited for something to happen, we noticed the curtain rods starting to sway back and forth. "They were not doing that before," I said. I checked to make sure that there was no heater or vent blower in that area. We noted on the video later at home that I had in fact bumped the curtain rod with my arm. Afterward, as we sat quietly on the couch, I could see the dots from the grid light moving on the ball in the hallway. "Is that ball moving right now?" I asked. No one was around it, but it seemed to be moving back and forth. We were able to catch the ball moving on video quite clearly.

We performed another EVP session, asking more questions to ascertain who might be there with us. By the time we were through, it was late. We were all tired so we decided to wrap it up for the night.

While going over my digital evidence, I found eleven more EVPs. One EVP was a man's voice and it sounded angry and curse words could be heard. The angry man clearly didn't like us being there in his space and asking questions. We also recorded an audible woman's voice again.

Better still was the strange, lighted orb right next to Martin's face while he was in the kitchen. It was the only picture I found while searching though my stack of photos with this lighted orb, so I could not debunk it. I am not big into orbs, but this one had a strange shape: Unlike dust or water, and it was right next to Martin's face.

I decided to contact a psychic medium to see what she would see or feel in the house. We had enough evidence now to convince me that there were spirits there. This family needed some closure and they wanted anything negative out of their dwelling. I was hoping the medium could help the family out and move any spirits on who needed to be crossed over into the Light.

I called a woman whose home we had previously investigated. She is not afraid of the paranormal, and now helps us out when we need it. Being a psychic medium, she can see and communicate with spirits and help them cross over.

When she arrived, I was setting up our evidence footage of the ball moving. I asked if she had picked up anything when she arrived. "Yes. As soon as I pulled into the driveway," she said. "I could see two female spirits standing in the driveway as if they were waiting for me to arrive here." This happens often as the psychic mediums begin getting a reading on the homes.

"Interesting," I said. "No one else?"

"Nope, just the two women. I don't see them now, though... Oh wait!" she said, "There is a man in the kitchen area, pacing back and forth. He looks very tense and agitated and very pissed off." She explained what he looked like to Martin. Looking nervous, he said, "You just described the guy who killed my ex-wife."

I was shocked, but judging by the sounds of the cursing

guy on the digital recorder, it made sense that my dowsing rods had indeed picked up his energy. I placed my new static box out in the kitchen area and it started flashing like crazy. It seemed that the killer was presently affecting it. The hair on my arms stood straight up, and I could really feel his negative energy in the kitchen area.

To have the psychic's opinion about evidence we had gathered, I put on the video clip of the ball moving back and forth. The medium said, "Oh, ghost guy just walked out here in the living room from the kitchen. He is looking at the TV and watching your video evidence now. He seems curious about it. "The angry guy is here in the room with us now?" I asked. Can you send him to the light?"

"Tell him yourself," she said. "He is listening to you and looking *right at you*."

I looked over at the TV area and asked the spirit to go to the Light, be at peace now, and leave this family alone. I said in a firm voice, "We know who you are so you need to leave this house now." It was really quiet after that so it made me wonder what was happening.

The medium said, "Oh, the two women standing in the driveway just walked into the kitchen area." She then described what the two women looked like in full detail. I looked at Martin and silently, we both agreed that the medium had just perfectly described Martin's deceased ex-wife.

"The other woman, I do not know. Who is she?" Martin asked.

"She is older." the medium explained.

"Maybe she's the killer's mother," I said.

"Well, that woman is now leaving with the bad guy, so maybe it is," the medium said as she watched them. "Yep, the man and the older woman just left the house, but the younger woman's standing right next to your daughter now."

The young daughter's eyes grew big. "Is that what I feel? I can feel her next to me," she said.

"Yes." the medium stated. "She has her hand over your hand."

"I can feel her, but she's cold." Then, the young girl put her hand up to the side of her face, with quite a shocked look on her face.

"Yes, your mom just kissed your cheek." the medium said.

Her eyes lit up. "Oh my God, I felt her kiss me." The daughter's eyes grew wider. We could tell that she was delighted because she had a big smile on her face as she teared up.

The dad said, "She never really knew her mom. She was little when her mom passed." I knew something very powerful was happening. I felt so much peace in the room. The room also seemed to be getting brighter. I will never forget the feeling that something special was happening.

"Your mom just walked over and sat down by you." the medium said.

The older daughter said, "Really?"

"She has a message for you. She watches over you and knows everything you do. She seems upset with your boyfriend/" the medium said.

The older daughter asked why.

"You started smoking because your boyfriend smokes and she does not like you smoking cigarettes." the medium said.

"That is true. I just started smoking last week."

"Yes. She knows that, and that's what she is telling you: She does not like it." The medium looked over at the younger daughter. "But she liked the project you just finished with planets," she said.

"I got a 98 on that project of the solar system." the little girl said.

"Yes, she has seen that and she is very proud of you." Then the medium looked over at the husband and said, "Your cooking is getting better, even though you cook mostly stew," she said. They all laughed and agreed that he does like to cook stew a lot, but it is pretty good. I could see the family getting the closure they really needed. It was a very peaceful feeling I will never forget. The mother's spirit was now by the older daughter. "She just wants you to know how proud she is of you." the medium said.

I asked if I could do a quick experiment. No one minded, so I put my static box next to the oldest girl on the couch. The medium started laughing a little. "What happened?" I asked.

"The mother spirit had her hand out, like she was going to take the box from you. You set it down on her lap and she is just looking at the box now." It was quiet, though; nothing was happening. "Can she set my static box off?" I asked.

The medium said, "She will try." Less than 10 seconds later, the static box started flashing very rapidly.

"Wow! She did it," I said. "She wanted to show you that she could make the box flash for you. She is happy she could do it for you."

The youngest daughter looked up and said, "I will never forget this night." It was very rewarding to see the family find some peace. "My sister and I witnessed something special that will always stay with me."

When I called back to check with the family, everything was quiet. The activity had completely stopped and the family was doing well. I was quite pleased to hear they were doing well and that we'd helped this family out.

I must say for all the skeptics out there that psychic mediums are real and do communicate with spirits. From what I have seen, psychic mediums give people a lot of peace and closure with their gift. It also takes many hours to go over evidence and investigate houses. Many people have no one to turn to as they do not want people feeling that they are crazy. So, they end up calling us with hope that we can help them out. We do not charge for our services. We would never want to feel like we were taking advantage of them. We have worked with many families and helped them gain some closure, explaining what was happening in their homes. However, this was such a cool story that it is one I will never forget.

OUIJA BOARDS

While growing up, we would play with my grandmother's Ouija board. We never felt any danger or were frightened by it. We actually got some pretty cool messages from the board. I have also heard some pretty scary stories about people inviting bad entities into their homes and then becoming terrorized by them. However, here is a good story that happened to us:

One day, we let our little puppy out to play in the yard. Not being very old, we tried to watch it to make sure that it didn't get out of our sight. However, when we turned around, the puppy was gone: We couldn't find it anywhere, despite the hours we spent looking. We figured it might get hungry and return home, however. Unfortunately, we were not that lucky.

Weeks went by and still, no puppy. We started to think we would never see the puppy again.

I'm not sure who brought it up, but someone said, "Hey! Let's ask the Ouija board where the puppy is." So, we sat down and asked the board where our lost puppy was or if it was still alive. The board said, "Yes, it is still alive." So, we asked where we would find the lost puppy.

The Ouija board started spelling out a road we knew pretty well. This road was many miles away, so we thought the board must've been wrong that our puppy had traveled that far. So, we asked the board again, but it kept spelling the name of the same road, over and over.

"Okay. Where on that road will we find the lost puppy?" we asked.

It quickly spelled out "by a green car."

We asked again, "Will we find the puppy by a green car?"

The pointer quickly shot to "yes."

We figured that we could take a drive to see if we could find our puppy. Honestly, we thought it was way too far for a little puppy to travel and it had been a couple of weeks that had passed. We did not think we would find the little thing alive, but it was a last ditch effort, so we drove out to the road. As we drove down the road, we did not see any animals or cars. We started to lose hope that we would ever see our puppy again.

"Wait!" someone said. "We just passed a green station wagon back there." So, we turned around and went back to the green station wagon.

As we pulled up, we did not see any movement, so we pulled over next to the green car. Just as we pulled over, we saw our puppy walk out from behind the green car. He looked very weak and skinny, but he was okay. We fussed over him, got him safely into the car, and back home.

So, in this story, working with the Ouija board was fine because our little puppy's life was saved. We still cannot believe the Ouija board sent us to the exact location where the puppy was at. We never had any problems using our board. Maybe we were protected by something? I do remember my psychic grandmother was one of the people using the board when we got the accurate information about our puppy so maybe that did help too.

We have also heard some bad stories resulting from Ouija board use, so I tell people not to play with them because they might bring unwanted spirits into their home.

One call was made to me after a group of teenagers had been playing with an Ouija board. The father called me and asked, "Is it true that you can open doors with an Ouija board?

I told my daughter not to play with it, but she did and now we are seeing dark shadows around our house. Doors are opening and closing by themselves, and we hear people talking at night when none of us are."

"Yes. I have seen this before, and yes: You can invite things into your house. You don't really know who you're talking to and it might be something bad. But you don't really know for sure."

"Great," the father said sarcastically. "Will it go away?"

"A lot of times it will go away on its own, if you firmly ask it to leave you alone and leave the house. When you're finished playing with the board you should say 'Goodbye.' This is only a theory of what to do but it seems to work."

In this case, they then asked whatever was in the house to leave and it seemed to work for this family because the activity ceased. The father then removed the board by throwing it away in the garbage. However, in other cases, I have seen the activity stay in the house. Sometimes, the families were tormented by what they had invited into their homes. It's not just a game so be careful of what you do.

In another situation, some young kids thought it would be cool to take their board to a nearby cemetery and communicate with the spirits there. They played with the Ouija board and started asking it various questions, but nothing really happened. So, they walked back home.

When they arrived there, the teenagers took the board upstairs to their room to try it again. This time, they asked if something had followed them home. The pointer quickly went to "yes" on the board. "Well, if that's true, prove to us that you're really here. Show us that you're here with us." they provoked it.

All of a sudden they heard a loud popping noise and all of the lights went dark in the house. The girls ran screaming downstairs, yelling for their dad to help them out. Their dad walked out of the living room and asked casually, "What did you guys plug in the wall outlet?"

"Nothing. We were playing with the Ouija board, though!" they yelled.

That didn't mean much to him. So, he went down into the basement to check the fuse box. What he found was pretty intense: All of the fuses had blown out in the fuse box. This had never happened before and he could not figure out what surged with enough power to blow out the fuses like that. One thing he did know though now that he was annoyed: He was throwing out the Ouija board and never allowing it in the house again.

The fuses never blew out like that again after getting rid of the board.

Another story I had heard about playing with the Ouija board was pretty frightening. A girl in her teens was playing around with an Ouija board and asking questions. She thought nothing would happen and she was correct, until later that night.

While she was sleeping, she was awoken by someone standing by her bed. She thought, "Okay. That's my brother playing around, trying to scare me." She looked closer at the figure and noticed that it was an older man who was quite scary-looking. She freaked out, scrambled out of bed, and ran to her parents' room crying.

She would sleep in her parents' room for months afterward because every time she returned to sleep in her bedroom, the man would appear out of nowhere and stand by her bed. It was almost a year before this man left her room. The last time she saw him, he was crouched down in one corner of the room. She screamed at him, telling him to leave her alone. This seemed to work because she never saw the man again. She never played with the Ouija board again as she did not want to invite anyone or anything like that into her house. So, be aware. The Ouija board is more than just a game. You can open up doors with it, bringing unwanted spirits into your home.

THE SATAN WORSHIPPER

Ghost Hunters of the Finger Lakes had received a call from another ghost hunting group asking if we wanted to investigate a house that they were not interested in doing. I said, "Okay. Is it local?"

"Yes, it's close to the area," he said. He gave me some details and told me that the clients had some negative forces in their house and they would not touch the investigation.

"Okay, sure. We never turn away anyone," I said. "We can check it out." I thought it was odd that they would give up an investigation because it sounded like a good one to check out. Later, I discovered that this case was turned down by several other groups because they felt that it was too negative to handle. I understood later what they were talking about.

We did not have a lot of time to do a walk-through first, but we knew it was a pretty small house, so we said we would just show up and investigate it. When I called them, they told me that whatever it was had followed them from one location to another. "This is not good," I thought. I got the feeling that they had probably messed with something bad or evil to bring this type of negative attachment to them.

They had had some personal items thrown off the counter and had seen a very scary-looking woman's face in their bathroom mirror. One night, they could hear something moving around in the living room. When they walked in, something dark was moving around and started growling at them. Then, in a quick flash, the dark shadow rushed at the man, knocking over a big recliner chair which was next to him. It really freaked him out. "One night, I heard someone talking. So I asked some questions with the phone recorder on." He actually had the equivalent of an EVP that was really loud on his phone, but it was hard to make out what it was saying. Either way, it did not sound human.

We quickly assembled and stationed our equipment to begin investigating the house. Suddenly, my EMF meter went off in the living room as my motion light flashed in the downstairs bedroom area. I decided to do an EVP session because we could see clearly on our cameras that no one was in there where my motion light went off. When I walked into the bedroom my stomach started to feel uncomfortable and uneasy. Then I noticed some unusual items in his room: a human looking skull and what looked like an animal coat with some sort of weird-looking head on it. As I got nearer to it, it made me feel nauseous and felt like I was going to puke.

"Hey! Oh, you found some of my old stuff. I used to use those while I was in this group," a man said behind me.

I turned quickly around. "What kind of group?" I asked.

"Well, it was not good. We were into Satan worshipping and had been involved in rituals. But, it was a long time ago. I got into trouble after that and started drinking and doing drugs. I even did some jail time. It was not good as I fell into this kind of dark stuff. Although I don't do that anymore, I still have some of the stuff we used to wear when we worshipped the Devil."

"That's not good. You may have opened yourself up to some extremely negative stuff, and I don't like this room," I said firmly. My motion light was still going off as we were talking and no one was near it. "Well, I would get rid of this stuff. It gives off a bad vibe. "I said.

When I played back my digital recorder, I heard an EVP

of a very deep dark and angry voice. The evil spirit cursed using the man's name. I do not feel comfortable repeating what he said, but I was not happy about it. I told him, "All I can say is: It is probably attached to you. I would get rid of the stuff you did your rituals with, especially the animal coat. It just creeps me out. I feel that there's something bad attached to that coat." I then played the EVPs I had caught in his house. He was pretty freaked out that we had caught a dark voice cursing and growling at him using his name.

"That's my name! Something's growling."

"Yes, it is and it does not sound good at all." I said. "It sounds inhuman to me and it's not good!"

The man cleaned up his room, tossing out all of the things he had kept from his satanic rituals. He mentioned that the room felt better when I spoke to him a couple of months later. However, he told me the following:

"I have to tell you what happened to me: About two weeks after I'd decided to leave this darkness behind me and throw out the items from the rituals, I had been involved in a very bad car accident. I almost died because I lost so much blood. I went into shock. They had two IV lines going into me, trying to replace the blood I had lost. You see, I severed a main artery in my leg and I should have died." I could not believe what he was telling me. Was this dark entity causing harm after he refused to be involved in the satanic practices? I was happy he was okay and he seemed to be getting better after this horrific accident.

I wonder to this day was this entity getting revenge on this man and caused the bad car accident? Even though He said the accident was not his fault: a car swerved and rammed into his car, causing the accident. He had since moved out of the house and seemed to be getting his life back together, so I was happy he had changed his ways. I always think that "good can always conquer evil" and in this case, it seems to have worked.

People should never mess with anything dark or do rituals that might open up negative attachments to them. As I write this, I have to wonder how many people have opened themselves up to dark forces and did not even know what they had done until it has been too late to save them from harm.

I always try to protect myself. You never know what you're up against. We try to stay away from provoking spirits or aggravating them needlessly. It is not smart to provoke something evil or tell it to do something to you.

When we first started doing investigations for the Ghost Hunters of the Finger Lakes, we did provoke spirits to push us, talk, show themselves, or do something to prove that they were there. One of our investigators did get pushed once as a result. It was interesting to see that some spirits could have that much power to do that. However, the investigator was very frightened that the spirit had pushed him, so we do not practice this much anymore. We never know who or what we are messing with until possibly later in the investigation and we do not want to ramp up the activity in the house, leaving the people worse-off than they were before we had investigated it.

THE HOUSE FROM HELL

We received a call from a family that needed help due to the things they were witnessing in their home. This was not a usual investigation as the activity was pretty extreme. I wanted to get a timeline starting at the actual beginning of the activity in the house. The family couldn't remember the exact starting point, but when there were some repairs done to the house. At first, it seemed that the home renovation seemed to disturb the spirits enough to set off the activity. They had lived in the house for six months previously and had not had any issues until that moment.

"All we did is replace a fan unit in the bathroom and vent," they said. They were not changing the house structure; the repair work was simple and minor.

"I don't think that's it." I said. "It has to be something else that caused this." They did speak to the neighbor next door, and mentioned that this was not the first family that had had this issue: Several families had moved in and out of the house. It seemed like an ongoing problem. I asked what was happening to them in the house.

The woman said, "Our front door will swing open in the middle of the night. We would lock the front door and later in the night it will just swing open and we can hear people walking around in the house. We can hear someone talking late at night in our bedrooms too. Our closet door will slide open and we see full body apparitions walking out of our closet. The kids are also having their closet door open, and apparitions walk out and stand next to their bed late at night. We can tell you it's not good, whatever is here.

We are getting pushed and held down in bed at night. I had to be rushed to the hospital a couple times because I thought I was having a heart attack. I woke up in my bed with extreme pain, and my heart was racing really fast. We called for an ambulance and they rushed me to the hospital that night. I felt like I was having heart attack. I had a bunch of tests done and they could not find anything wrong with me. The second time, I felt like something was holding me down in my bed.

I thought it was just me until my sister spent the night here and slept in my bed. My sister woke up with something pushing her down in the bed and said that her heart felt like it was coming out of her chest. She said, 'What the hell is wrong with your house? I felt like I was having a heart attack in your bed!' Then, I knew that it wasn't just me having the attacks while sleeping in my bed. The other night, my husband felt something grab his arm while we were sleeping. He said it felt like a dog was biting his arm and he could hear growling noises while this happened. He said, 'My arm actually rose up into the air while something was biting it and shaking my arm back and forth in the air. I actually had bite marks on my arm right after the attack. It scared the hell out of me.' he told me."

I could tell this family was really frightened and wanted some answers to what was happening in the house. The woman continued, "We just want some proof that we are not crazy and this is really happening. Our kids tell us there is a family of spirits here and they talk to them. Our kids say the spirits told them they live in the attic. We hung crosses up on the walls to protect us from whatever is here in the house. The next day, our kids said, 'Mom, the spirits don't like the crosses up on the wall. The spirits said we better take them down right away.' The next day the crosses had been flipped upside down by something."

Some red flags shot up as this did not sound good at all. I tried to make sense of it and thought, "Well, maybe the spirits were not of a religious background and did not like the crosses on the wall." At the same time, I thought it could be demonic or something inhuman as that would make more sense. I got the feeling that whatever it was seemed to be disguising itself and was not showing what it really looked like. These entities can be known as shape shifters as they can take form of anything they think you might feel safe seeing. Usually a young girl spirit or boy can be seen, and they try to make contact in some way, but it is really not a human spirit. At this point Ghost Hunters of the Finger Lakes had never had a case this negative, so we had to be careful with the handling of it. We needed to protect ourselves before we investigated this house.

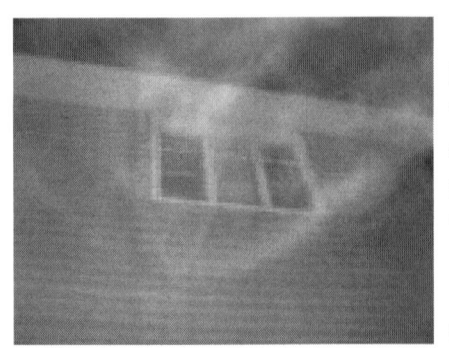

The family had taken a photo of the house with a huge, white mass around it. I asked if anyone had been smoking at the time the photo was taken. They said, "No."

No one was in the house at the time this photo was taken. The swirling mist was gone in the next photo taken less than a few seconds later.

It was hard to figure out what it was, but I did not get a good feeling about the house. I picked up some holy water at a nearby church and brought that over along with several crosses for protection. I sent the photo of the house to a medium friend of mine to see what she could read off of it.

I work nights so I thought I would take a long nap before we investigated the house. I thought I would need to be awake and alert on this investigation. As I was sleeping I had the craziest dream about the house we were going to investigate. I was fighting off something very evil-looking and I kept yelling at it to get away from me. All I remember was that it was an ugly-looking creature that was in no way a human form. It had claws and wavy tentacle-like arms and it seemed very powerful too. The inhuman-looking creature seemed to be threatening harm to me as it got closer. I remembered screaming for the evil looking creature to get away from me! I woke up sweating and breathing heavily, and thinking, "What the Hell just happened?" My pillow was soaked from sweating profusely. I thought to myself, "I don't ever have dreams like that."

My wife walked by the bedroom and said, "Are you alright?"

I said, "I just had the craziest dream ever."

She said, "I know. I could hear you screaming at something to get away from you."

"You heard that?" I asked.

"Yes. You were screaming at something," she said. I told her about the dream. She just said her usual, "You'd better not ever bring anything home with you. I don't like the sound of that."

I described what I saw and felt to a local artist who created a painting of the inhuman entity standing over me while I was sleeping. It had sharp claws, red eyes, and tentacle-like arms.

Later, investigators told me that if we investigate something evil or demonic, we will get a sign before investigating there. It made me wonder what we were dealing with. Just before I was leaving to investigate, I got a message and warning from the psychic medium I had sent the photo to. She said, "You know that photo you sent me the other day? Whatever it is can be very negative, so be careful tonight when investigating that house. We had activity in our house all night after you sent that photo to us. We had books fly off the table and we heard growling noises in our closets all night and heard something moving around in there." She continued, "I had a vivid dream last night that you and I were fighting off something dark and evil-looking creature." The dream was very similar to mine. It made me think about what would cause dreams like that. Is it a coincidence that two different people had almost the exact same dream?

I was thankful for the warning as I had my equipment packed and ready to go. It was couple of hours away, so I had to get moving. We met at our usual place and I told our investigators what had happened. "We must be careful on this one as I don't get a good feeling about this house." The other investigators agreed we should be careful.

When we arrived at the house, the family seemed pretty tense. "We did not even want to sleep upstairs last night," they said. They would not go into full detail about what they'd encountered the night before. "We are not staying here while you investigate. Only my older son will stay with you. We are not sure we can handle this," they said.

I asked, "What has happened in the house lately?"

"Well, I woke up with scratches down my inner thigh area," the lady said. "We have been getting pushed down the stairs, and now they are scratching us." she said. We asked what the scratches looked like and were told that all of the scratches were grouped into three long scratch marks each, indicating that the apparition may have had only three fingers or claws on each hand. The lady continued, "So, we will not be here tonight while you investigate. Good luck, and I hope you find something here but we will not join in any part of it." she said.

As I walked upstairs, I got a very negative feeling, almost like whatever was in the house did not want us there. All of the investigators felt the same intense feeling, but we continued on anyway. We had all the bedrooms wired with video and ran all the wires downstairs to our TV monitors. We had motion lights pointing toward the closets where the family had said the closet doors would open up at night. We tried to debunk the closet doors opening up, but I not could see any way these closet doors would open by themselves as they seemed to lock into place and were difficult to open. I had my portable camera in the basement with another motion light set up. I started walking upstairs when I felt a very strong energy. The hair on my arms stood straight up. I yelped, "Wow! We need to hang out up here and just observe to see what we could hear." We could clearly hear someone walking down the main hallway, so I quickly asked if anyone of our investigators was walking around.

"No." they said. They were sitting still.

I asked whatever was there to make a noise for us. Right then, I heard a loud tap on the window right above my head in the kids' room. It was a two story house and there were no trees, or anything else, close enough to the window to make that noise on it. We did an EVP session, conducted an EMF sweep, and found no EMFs whatsoever. So, we walked back downstairs and thought we would just watch the TV monitors for any activity.

The family's son said, "You need to come over here and check this out!" He had been watching the TV monitors very closely. "Watch the motion lights pointed in at the closets." he said. Where the motion lights were pointing inside the closets there was a wall divided the two bedrooms. "Whatever that was walked through the wall and into the other bedroom." the son said.

It did seem that way due to motion lights going off, which were pointed directly into the closets. The motion lights had an infrared beam shooting out in the closet. The only way for the motion light to be tripped was if something was physically breaking the beam from the motion light. I said, "It went on several times." Then the other bedroom motion light went on. Two of us decided to go up there alone and just lay in the bed for a while to see what happens. It was also where the family member had been scratched. As I walked upstairs, I began to feel light-headed and then felt a presence there. I had my EMF meter, so I thought I would check the kids' bedrooms for any changes in the EMF field. As soon as I walked into the bedroom, the meter spiked very high EMFs, so I radioed down that I was getting very high EMFs in the kids' bedroom.

This picture was taken by me with my full-spectrum camera showing the EMF meter light up on the left side of the picture. Our EMF meters were going off in the kids' bedroom near the same closet in which motion lights had been triggered by something in the closet. This is also the same closet that had a door which would open up at night. The children could see spirits walking out of it and standing by the kids' beds to stare at them. I recorded the motion light activity earlier.

It went away in less than a minute. I was upstairs alone, so I thought I would lie down in the bed that the mother had been scratched and held down in. Nothing happened, so I laid there in bed with my digital recorder, going near the closet. With my digital recorder running, I asked if anyone was in the bedroom with me. What I didn't realize yet was that there was a ghost yelling at me. I got a response from what sounded like an angry older lady. She yelled, "What are you doing here!

There was a lot of activity going on in this home. The other investigator played back his digital recorder, which he had going when he opened up the attic door. It sounded like someone made a comment to him and you could hear a lot of whispering going on. When going over my video in the basement, I got several motion light hits. Something was moving around in the basement. The video showed that there was nothing setting off the motion light. At one point, I thought I'd caught a shadow, but it was hard to make out. My sister decided to lay in the bed upstairs by herself to discover if anything would happen to her. We got a very big orb over her while she was in the bed. I have mixed feelings about orbs, but it was taken with a night vision camera and no flash on, so it meant more to us than it would have if we had used a normal camera.

The orb on the top right of the photo seemed to be hovering over my sister's head. A psychic medium told me she thought it was a protective spirit and nothing evil in any way. We did ask for protection before we entered the home so it makes sense.

I called the family back after I had finished going over the evidence there. "I want to show you what we caught there."

"Well, you're going to have to show us at another house. We moved out last week," she said. I asked what happened. "We were all scratched!" The older son woke up with a burning sensation on his leg.

"I fell asleep with my jeans on," he said. "When I took off my pants, I had three long claw marks going down the back of my leg. It really burned." he said. The other kids were scratched, too. "They all had three long scratch claw marks on them," they told me.

The lady continued, "As I went upstairs, my back started burning, and right after that, the middle of my back had three long scratch marks appear on it."

Later, I was told that the three long scratch marks could be evil, and a trinity sign from the Devil. I was thinking about this when I was talking to the owner. "Wow!" I said, "But you're alright now?"

"Well, we're out of the house from Hell." she said. "We can at least sleep at night now. We would not go upstairs the last couple days we spent in the house. Every time we did, we would feel the burning sensation on our backs. We knew what would happen if we stayed up there. We did not want to be scratched again." she said. "We all slept downstairs in the kitchen area as we refused to go back upstairs." she said. "We will never go near that evil house from Hell again! "That house should be demolished." they said. "No one should ever live in that house as it's evil!"

When I played the evidence for them, we caught growling noises and spirits talking to us. The motion lights were going off when no one was upstairs or downstairs in the basement. They were pleased to know that they were not crazy or imagining it. They said, "Wow! There was something really bad in that house!" The family was still very nervous and concerned. "Will it follow us to our next house?" they asked.

I did not want to scare them even more. I said, "Most of the time the spirits stay with the house and I'm really hoping this will be the case for you."

"Will it matter what kind of house we get?"

"Is that the only house you experienced activity in?" I asked.

"Yes, that is the only place we ever had that happen to us. We never believed in that stuff until that happened." she said.

"I don't think it's attached to you." I said. "I think it's staying in the house but it will be hard to get rid of." I was hoping this family would not have any other issues in their new home, especially after everything they had been through.

The family moved very far away. Naturally, they wanted no part of that house ever again. When I called back a few months later, they reported that they were okay and had had no other issues after moving. They told me that they would feel sorry for whoever moved into that house next.

Five months went by. Then, I received a call from a person that wanted to talk about a house that had a lot of activity in it. "You've already investigated this house." he said. "We've had doors open on their own, and we can hear people talking at times."

My heart sunk in my chest as he told me the address of the house. I knew it was the same house that the other family had moved out of. I knew I had to do something this time to try to rid whatever was there in the house. The Ghost Hunters of the Finger Lakes went back to the house with a psychic medium. She said, "Something inhuman is here in this house." She felt sick and had to leave the house to regain her composure. She could feel a negative presence there, as well as other spirits. She said, "Some kids who were doing rituals in the basement had invited something bad into the house. It will be hard to close this off as it's really strong here."

She had us recite some protection prayers, hoping they would help. I also gave prayer cards to the owners of the house and the rest of the family to help keep them protected.

The activity seemed to calm down for a while. But later, when I checked with the family again, something had happened in the house. The mom said, "I could sense something was upstairs by me. I walked over to the top of the stairs and started telling my kids something. I could feel two hands on my back. Then, some unseen force pushed me down the stairs. I landed at the bottom." she said. "I did not want to scare my kids, so I told them, 'Mommy is alright. I just slipped.' A few weeks later, I also watched my daughter slide down the same stairs. I thought she was playing around, but my daughter said, 'Someone helped me down the stairs, Mommy. I felt their hands in my back.' The very next day, my other daughter was pushed down the stairs. No one was hurt, but it scared us." she said.

This case is ongoing. We plan to revisit the house and try to help the family out there.

THE GHOST IN THE WINDOW

 I visited a very old museum just out of the area. As I toured the museum, they told me about many encounters with what they referred to as the original owner of the museum. "He likes to play games with us." they said. "One day, we were locked out of the museum when we stepped outside for a few minutes. There are eyehooks on the inside of the doors. Someone had latched the eyehooks inside while everyone was standing outside of the museum." I checked the old eyehooks: There was no possible way that could have happened by accident. The museum staff told me, "That's not all. We have had books fly off the shelves and things move in here." I was very interested, so I asked to come back and investigate the old museum.

 It was winter time, the weather was bad, and the weather men were calling for more snow. I decided to tough it despite the 5-8 inches of snow that we got hit with that night. None of the other investigators could make the trip, so I set off alone with a few video cameras and my digital recorder. Hours later, I still didn't have any video evidence or EVPs. However, I did have a few EMF hits downstairs in the living room area. As I walked in the kitchen, I snapped off a couple of pictures with my regular camera. What I got was a very unusual photo of what appeared to be a ghost-like feature in the window. It seemed to have a face with eyes. I could not debunk this photo even though I went back to check if there was a reflection or some kind of poster that had reflected in the window when I took the picture. I could not duplicate the photo, despite the many different camera angles I used to try to recapture the photo I got that night. You decide for yourself as you look at this photo.

If you look just below the pointed mist at the top middle of the photo, you may see a face in it. The mouth is open and the ghost's tongue is even visible as a white blob in the middle of the blackness, just above the top ridge or line in the middle of the window. There seems to be a second face in the bottom right hand corner of the photo too. The eyes and nose are very clearly defined.

FACE IN THE MIRROR

A lady contacted me about some activity she was having in her house in the area. When I arrived, the lady had just gotten out of work and pulled into the driveway. She said, "You go first." as she handed me her house keys.

I thought, "That was odd." but said, "Okay."

I pushed on the front door to the house. As I opened the front door, there seemed to be something up against it. The lady noticed I had felt that and said, "See? That's what happens to me all the time. People think I'm crazy, but you can see what happens now."

I said, "Yes. Is someone home now?"

"No," she said, "My roommate is not in town this weekend and there is only one entrance to the house. I live upstairs."

I looked behind the door. There were kitchen bowls and other things, stacked up against the door. "That stuff is from the kitchen area." she said. "Something is here 'cause I've witnessed many things. Whatever it is hides my car keys in different places. I have made many different sets as my keys come up missing a lot. I usually find them in my shoes, the garbage cans, and even the toilet! Places where I would obviously never put them."

About a month later, her roommate told me he had witnessed a dark shadow figure walking by him while he was watching TV. He said, "The man was solid black and wore a hat. The shadow man walked right over and looked directly at me, then turned around and walked out into the kitchen area. He disappeared into the kitchen wall as I was watching him. Every hair on my arms rose up, and I felt an electric charge in the room when this happened. I never believed in this stuff, but this scared the shit out of me and now I believe in ghosts." he said, apparently freaked out as he relived the incident for me.

The lady of the house then mentioned that a woman may have overdosed on some drug and died in the house. She had heard a spirit girl talking about this and how she died. The spirit girl would also come to her in her dreams. The lady also mentioned that the lights had at times flickered on and off. Her kitchen appliances would turn on and off as well. "I have had my radio and TV both turn on by themselves." she said.

The Ghost Hunters of the Finger Lakes team decided to return back to the house later to do an investigation there. We started out about 4 o'clock in the evening and when we arrived, began setting up our video and audio equipment. When we had the audio and video running, we remembered that we had forgotten to feed the parking meters so we decided to go back to put some quarters in them so we would not get a parking ticket.

When I got to my truck, I looked on the front seat and around the inside floor for more quarters. I said to myself, "Oh great! Now I will probably get a parking ticket."

"I could use some help here," I said jokingly, out loud. I looked back up to the front seat area, and there, three quarters were lying on the front seat!

"Where did they come from?" I asked myself. It was really strange to see them there because I had just looked at the front seat area very carefully before searching the rest of the car. "I guess someone is helping me out today," I said to the air.

The other investigator met up with me at the house. He mentioned that something usual had also happened to him. "What happened?" I asked.

"Well, I needed quarters for the meter and I could not

find any. I looked inside my car, but did not find any there either." he said. "I had a couple of dimes and walked back over to the meter to put the dimes in it. When I did, I noticed a bunch of quarters lying on the ground next to the meter. I know for a fact that the quarters were not there before."

"That's really strange, 'cause I had a similar experience." I told him.

As we were investigating the living room area, I could feel something touching the back of my neck. It was very faint, but definitely there. The other investigator could feel it also. "You feel that?" I asked him.

"It just felt like something was touching my neck." he said.

The hair on my arms stood on end again. "Man, it feels like something is here!" I said. My EMF meter, sitting on the table, started to go off. We recorded some very high EMFs in the room. When we'd recorded enough to be satisfied that we had a ghost with us, I asked if there was anything they wanted to tell us before we put the equipment away.

After the investigation, we returned to my house to go over the findings. I found a very interesting EVP of a young girl talking on my digital recorder. She was mumbling a lot, so we could not tell what she was saying. She sounded drunk, high, or very out of it. Then, I remembered that the lady had said that there had been a woman who may have died due to an overdose of drugs. That statement made sense given what was on the EVP.

Only one statement was clear: I heard a very loud, "Get out!" right after I asked if anyone was with us. When I went over my evidence, I found a very interesting photo of what looked like an old Native American face in one of the mirrors. I started checking the history in that area and found out some interesting facts: While workers were digging basements in the area where this house was built, they found some Native American bones. They noted that the bones were a charred reddish color which had apparently occurred after ritual cremation ceremonies to honor and release the spirits of loved ones who had passed away.

I went back to the lady's house to show her what evidence of apparitions we had found there. While I was waiting in her living room area, a radio started to play music very loudly. No one was physically around the radio, so I thought it was very odd that it came on by itself.

The lady walked out to the living room and looked at the radio. "Did you turn the radio on?" she asked.

"No, I just walked in here." I said.

"That's not the first time this has happened to me." she said. "The TV has turned off and on by itself, too," she explained again. I showed her the photo that was taken of her bedroom mirror. She was quite shocked. She threw the old mirror out after I showed her the photo. "There was no I was way keeping that mirror!" she said. "I never liked that mirror anyways; it always creeped me out."

"Maybe that's why you were creeped out by the mirror."

Because the lady had experienced many things she could not explain in her home, she eventually moved out and seemed a lot happier after doing so. I think the house had a negative spirit in it. Later, I heard from one of my psychic friends that she had been told by the Native American spirits in her area that "nobody should live on an Indian burial ground" because it upsets the spirits buried there and can cause the living to have difficulties.

GHOSTS ARE REAL

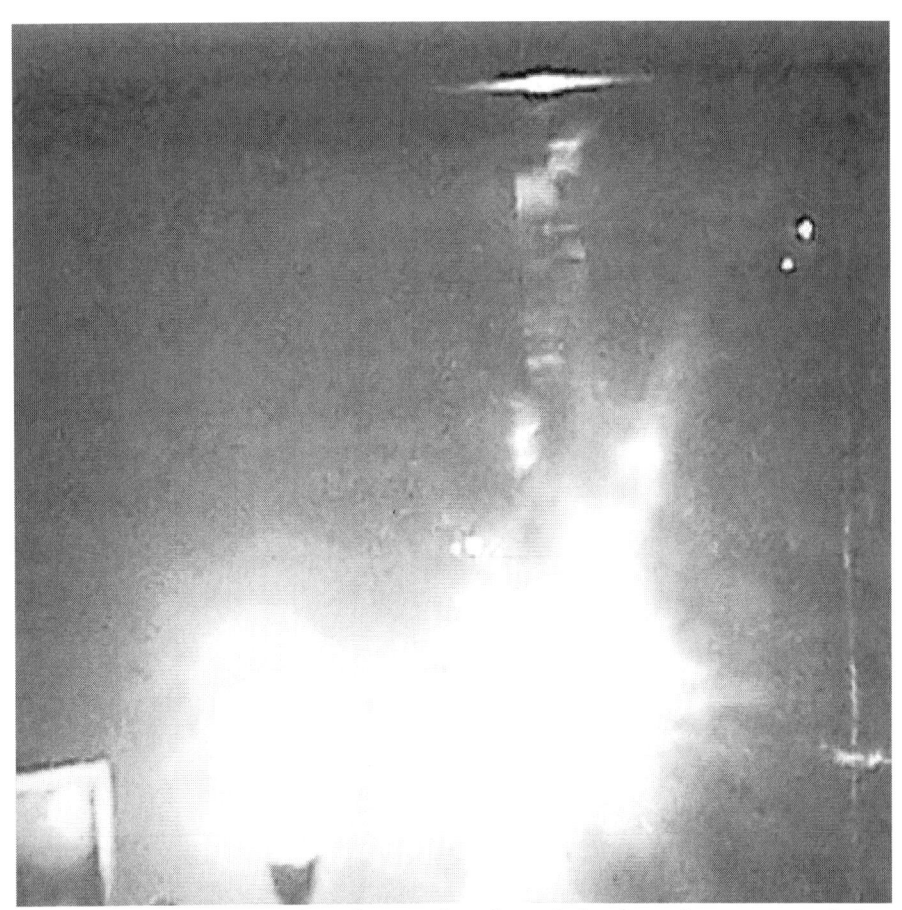

If you look closely up in the right hand corner of the photo from that house, you might be able to see a face. Some think it is a Native American face in the mirror. I will let you be the judge. Can you see the face in the mirror?

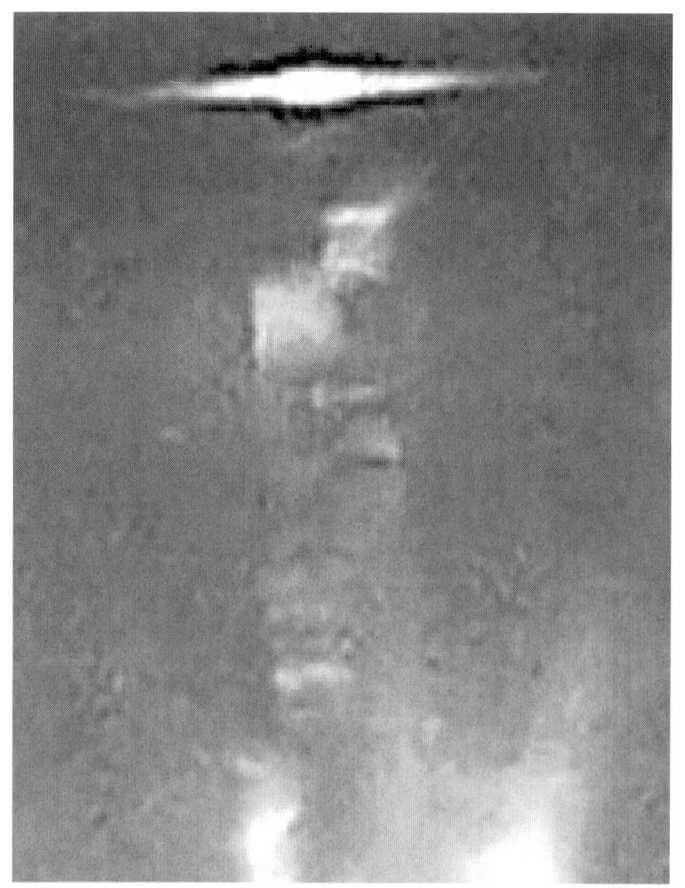

The same photo, except that I zoomed in more on the face. You can see the light portal open at the top of this photo. I have seen this light several times in my spirit photos. My theory is that the portal is there to allow spirits to travel through. Mirrors also hold energy. Some people say they can see a medallion on the forehead and a Native American headdress and war paint on the face. I'll let you decide what you see in this photo.

A FRIEND'S HOME

A friend of mine said, "Oh, you should investigate my house. I grew up in this house and know something is there. I've witnessed many things I cannot explain. I have heard doors opening by themselves, footsteps down the hallway late at night, and I have heard weird scratching noises inside my bedroom closet door late at night. But, just the other day, my dad saw a huge black shadowy person down in the basement. He actually walked up to it and put his hand right through it. He was large, black, and misty. The black mist vaporized right before his eyes."

"Wow! That's pretty interesting." I said. So we agreed on a time to meet at the house to set up the equipment. I had my dowsing rods ready, and they pointed to a table where we had a TV monitor set up. Through the use of "yes" or "no" questions, the dowsing rods helped us to determine that we had found a man from the late 1800s. "Interesting: my dowsing rods crossed which indicated I have a man here in the living room. The monitors are showing that motion lights are going off in the bedroom closet which is where the energy is." I said.

"That's the closet where I heard the scratching when I was a kid." she said.

"Wow! It seems like there is something here."

We continued the investigation. There were strange noises in the kitchen area. The dog started to bark at whatever the noise was in there. Every time I checked, there was no physical person there. Just then, my EMF meter, sitting on the table, started to flash. My dowsing rods pointed to the kitchen and then to the dining room table where the EMF meter was going off.

I had invited another woman that we knew who was very open to spirits and could actually see spirits rather than only hear or feeling them. I thought it would be good to have her go along and see if she picked up anything while she was there in the house. I asked her what she was picking as she made a nervous face while she looked at the same table where the EMF meter was flashing. She stated, "There is a huge spirit guy standing over there by that table every time you walk by him he makes a face at you like what are you doing here? I think he may have been a farmer. He has a huge hat on his head too,: she said.

"It's like it's his house and he doesn't want you are here and he is making his presence known." I said, and quickly set up my motion camera also pointing at the table where the activity seem to happening.

It was interesting to get high EMFs while having a psychic see the spirit and my dowsing rods pointing to the same exact spot where this spirit was standing. I thought it was good to have actual scientific evidence along with what the sensitive person had seen and what my dowsing rods were picking up. I could not wait to get home and go through my evidence and see what was captured.

When I went over the photos from the investigation later that night, I got some very unnerving images. When we were picking up our TV monitors, something began to materialize in the photos. At first, it seemed like a body of a person, but it grew in size. We accidentally walked right through it as if it was not there because we couldn't see it. It was also right where the psychic had seen the big spirit and where my dowsing rods pointed and EMF meter was going off by the table.

GHOSTS ARE REAL

This is a picture of my sister, Patti, picking up a TV monitor. You can see the body in front of her starting to appear. The body has no head and my sister seems to be walking right through it. You can see my sister's reflection in the window, but you cannot see the strange, headless body reflected. The owners were home and sitting in the living room at the same time this picture was snapped so we had many witnesses to no one being there with us while this photo was taken.

If you look at the time stamp of the first photo, it shows that it started at 10:19 pm. Two minutes later at 10:21 pm, the spirit was fully formed with a head. In the next photo the apparition had a head, and appeared to be wearing a three-pointed hat on its head, like the ones worn back in the late 1800s. The owners were shocked when I showed them this photo.

This is another photo of the same location that the large entity was found in. I could not debunk this. It looks as if the figure also had a hat on just as in the previous two photos. He also appears to be moving and hunched over. This house had a lot of activity in it, so it could have been someone other than the farmer, a second entity. I will let you form your own opinion on this. We did hear plenty of noise from the kitchen area that night and could not tell where the noises were coming from. The family dog also started barking, letting us know that something was in the kitchen. Do you think that the dog could see and sense the spirit man? The psychic also said there was more than one spirit from what she could see.

THE HAUNTED BAR

We had already investigated some houses just outside of our hometown when a couple of people told us about a really old bar that had a lot of paranormal activity in it so we thought we'd better stop by to ask if the bar workers had any ghost stories they could share with us.

We walked in, obviously ourselves. Before we'd even asked any questions, a drunk guy at the bar said, "Hey! You know this bar is haunted, right?"

We just looked at each other before looking back at the bar guy. Then, I said, "Really? What happens here?"

The bar guy did not speak as I think he had put a few beers away already, so the bartender began to tell us about a shadowy figure many workers had seen there. The shadowy figure had a hat on and was solid black. "I watched him walk into the kitchen area. I thought it was another worker until I realized that he [the other worker] was outside at the time. The ghost just walked back in the bar. We looked around in the kitchen area, but found out that no one was there. It was kind of spooky because I'd seen the shadow man with my own eyes." he said.

"What else goes on here?" I asked.

"Well, sometimes our receipt machine prints out random messages on it. It's not supposed to do that as it only prints numbers," he said. "One day was really scary because the ghost seemed to know what was going around here."

"Like how?" I asked.

"Well, we heard some sirens going off and thought that

there'd been a bad accident nearby the bar. It seemed to be just around the corner. We were all wondering what had happened. Well, we have a big billboard at the front of the bar over there and the words on it are programmed for us. But that day, the words started changing on the billboard. They went from the menu specials to 'kill, kill, kill.' No one had touched the board or had messed with it. We were pretty freaked out. I walked over to turn the billboard off and the original words flashed back on the billboard. We later found out that someone had been shot and killed at the same time the board was flashing 'kill' on it. We wondered if something was warning us not to go outside or just telling us what was happening."

Another story he told was the following:

"We could hear some noise upstairs in the storage room. One day, the noise was really loud, so we decided to see what it was. As we opened the door at the top of the stairs, we could see an old rocking chair, rocking back and forth. We could also hear some kids giggling. We quickly went back downstairs and did not stick around to see anything else. Another time, we went upstairs to get something out of the storage room. When we looked at the window, we could see a face in it! It was on the second floor, so there was no way that a person could have been looking through that window. It feels creepy upstairs, so when we go up there, we don't stay too long."

While investigating the old bar, I set my EMF meter on the table and then continued to ready the other equipment. There were a few people in the bar, watching us work. One guy pointed to my EMF meter and said, "That instrument is going off just after you walk right by it, every time."

I thought it was strange, so I watched it after I walked by the meter. Sure enough, the meter started flashing every time I passed by it.

"Whatever it is it seems to be following you." the man said.

"Yes, it does. That meter has never done that."

It was very strange. We witnessed many high EMF readings throughout the bar. All of which were attributable to paranormal activity except those around a few electrical outlets. Then my dowsing rods pointed upstairs, so we walked up to the second floor.

The hair on my arms instantly shot up and I experienced that weird feeling of knowing that there was something or someone around us. "Wow! I feel it up here." I said. My dowsing rods instantly crossed, meaning that there was a high energy spot there. I had another investigator hold the EMF meter under my dowsing rods at where they had crossed. The EMF meter instantly started flashing, showing high EMFs right where my dowsing rods had just crossed. It was quick, though, and the meter stopped flashing in just a few seconds as the energy quickly dissipated.

I continued taking pictures through the bar areas. I noticed a bigger difference in the second photo than in the first one. I looked back to the first and noticed that there seemed to be a face in it. The second photo just showed a window.

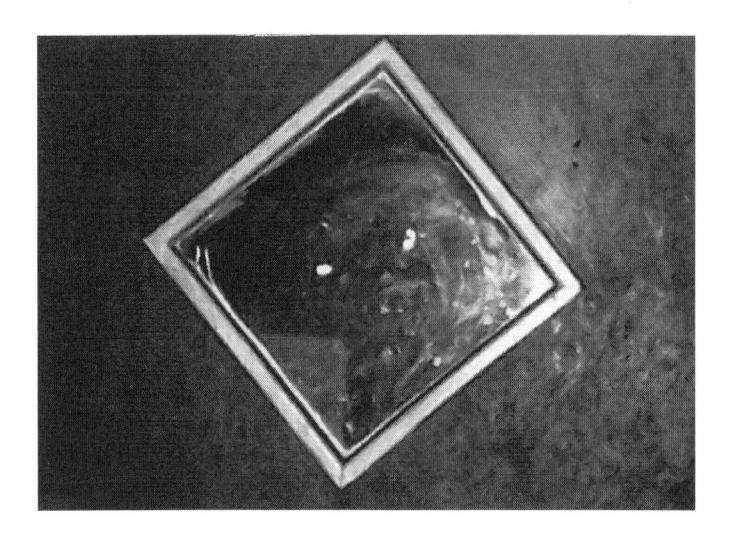

This is the photo of the door window. Some people can only see smudges in it. Others can see a face. Some people have said that the face reminds them of a bear. Some think it is evil. I will leave it up to you to let you form your own opinion on it.

WILLARD ASYLUM

One day, we decided to go on an open tour in Willard asylum. We thought it would be a good idea to learn about the old buildings there, and of course, look for ghosts while we were at it. As we toured the old buildings, I felt a sensation that I will never forget.

I had just entered Hadley Hall, which was a very old theater that was built back in 1892 on the Willard asylum property. The residents would put on plays, practice their music, and do many other activities. When I entered the Hadley Hall building, I was feeling okay. However, as I walked to the main floor, I started feeling funny. I kept looking at the back part of the theater, thinking that this place was odd. So, I walked over to the backstage where there were ropes and pulleys to control the curtains. I got a cold chill with goose bumps on my arms.

I had just purchased a full-spectrum camera and wanted to try it out.

Note: a full spectrum camera is a camera that is especially built with the filter removed that blocks most spectrums of light, thus allowing for a full-spectrum of light. Many investigators believe the filters block out what we cannot see with our own eyes making these cameras better for ghost hunting.

I knew something was there as I could feel it. It almost felt like it was watching me so I looked-up at the balcony and thought, "This is where I am getting this feeling from."

I snapped many pictures of the balcony and surrounding areas. I knew no one was in the balcony, as the steps were closed off and there was no way up there. The chills stopped then, and

I did not feel anything more so I continued on with the tour. However, I knew something strange had just happened there.

When I got home, I quickly went over the photos I had taken at Willard. As I looked at the balcony photos, I noticed that one picture stood out. Something seemed to be in the photo, but in the next photo, it was not there. I zoomed in on one and could not believe what I saw. A lady in a white dress looking down at me from the balcony! She seemed to be wearing a hat and glaring out at me from behind it. The photo validated exactly what I had felt, that there was someone watching me from the balcony.

Here is the woman standing on the balcony. This beautiful ghostly lady with the long tent-like dress was caught with my full spectrum camera. That's why she has a different color than the rest of the picture does. If you look to the right-hand corner, you should be able to find her. She's standing on the far right-hand side of the balcony. Can you see what I see? Some people have a hard time seeing this figure. It looked to me as if the lady had make-up on as her face because it looks lighter that it should. There were many deaths in this asylum Many patients had taken their own lives. Staff were not trained in handling people with mental health issues in this time, and often treated them more like prisoners than patients. On the tour they told me people have heard music still playing in the Hadley hall theatre at times.

THE SENECA FALLS HOUSE

The Ghost Hunters of the Finger Lakes received an e-mail from a very stressed-out woman asking for help: "Please help us. We are having a lot of activity in our house." She was pregnant at the time, and she had a 2-year-old daughter who also had seen things in the house. "The house we live in is very active, and we have been experiencing many things in it. The kid's toys start playing for no reason in the middle of the night. Something touched me and pulled at my pillow one night. I even had my hair pulled by something. One time my boyfriend and I saw a man in a black cape or robe. It was very jagged and whoever he was, he seemed very evil. My daughter talks to something, but we cannot see who she is talking to. My daughter said it's a little girl who talks to her. The little girl spirit also likes to play with my daughter's toys too. . The little spirit girl also likes to plays games with my daughter. When I ask my daughter who she is playing with, she says it's the little girl playing with me."

I asked the lady is she had any traumatic deaths in the family or any other events that may be connected to her. "Yes. I know someone who died from a suicide." she said. "But that was about ten years ago. It was very tragic and it affected me a lot. The activity has been going on for a while now, but it's really bad now and it's never been this bad. Wherever I go it seems to follow me. Whatever it is, it's causing me a lot of stress. One night, it even scratched me and pushed down on my legs. I was very frightened because I'm not sure what it is. Whatever it is needs to leave me alone."

I knew we needed to follow up right away to help them. I asked her if she always felt spirits around her and she responded, "Yes, I have."

I thought, "Well, maybe she is sensitive; pulling in the spirits as they know she can feel them around her." I also wondered if being pregnant was also making things worse. I thought it was important to get out there right away and see what we could do to help this family out.

We arrived and assessed the house to find the best place to set up our equipment. I turned on my motion camera and pointed it down the hallway while we set up our other equipment.

While the equipment was being stationed and prepared to activate, we realized we had forgotten some important plugs for our recorders and had to go back to get them. I looked at the lady and her boyfriend and asked if they knew how to record EVPs. "Yes, we watch the ghost shows." she said. I turned on one of my portable cameras and pointed at them. I said, "Go ahead and ask some questions, and we will return back with the power cords."

When I did return, I found both of them pretty excited. "We did what you said and we actually heard voices."

"You got some voices on the recorder?" I asked. "No, we actually heard a little girl talking to us on your voice recorder. We caught the voices in the kids' room." I had previously asked them if they could find a babysitter while we were investigating. I was glad they did, and there were no children in the home at the time of the paranormal investigation.

When I played back the recorder, I could hear a little girl's voice on it. "Yep, sounds like a small girl is here. We didn't tell you yet, but whatever is here keeps setting the rocking horse off late at night," she said. "You have to pinch the ear on the rocking horse and then it makes a loud horse sound. We hope the rocking horse goes off for you guys tonight."

I quickly set up cameras on the rocking horse so that I would get the sound and any other activity on video if it did go off on its own. As I set my video camera up, it felt really heavy and dark in the kid's room. "Wow! I feel the energy in here." I said. "It does not feel good in here at all."

"This is my daughter's room and where she talks to the spirits." the lady said. "It scares my daughter now. She does not like the little girl, she says she is bad. I did not tell you about the other night I put some laundry in the dryer while I was here alone, but when I returned to get the laundry out, the laundry was gone! I still haven't found the laundry yet. It's disappeared." she said. "It still freaks me out that something took my laundry." she said. "No one could have possibly walked in the room without me hearing them."

We continued investigating, listening for any sounds or voices. I had just set up a grid light in the daughter's bedroom to catch ghosts in the hallway when I put my flashlight off and pointed down in the doorway with the lens facing the floor. I sat down on the couch and we just sat there for a while, listening in silence. All of the sudden, we heard something topple over. Then, a light turned on in the hallway. I said, "Can you see the light now in the hallway?"

One of the investigators watching the TV monitors said, "Yes I see it but I can't tell what exactly what it is. There is a light on in the hallway that wasn't that way a minute ago as I've been watching the monitors this whole time." he said. So, I cautiously walked down the hallway to see where the light was coming from. I looked down and noticed that my flashlight had been knocked over and was now turned on and shining brightly. I said, "What the heck?" and reached down to pick it up. As soon as I did this, the rocking horse right next to me started to go off. I have to say that it startled me, and I jumped back. I could feel the strong presence was in the room with me.

I could not believe what had just happened; I was shocked and mumbled something unintelligible even to myself. The investigator watching the monitor had seen everything and had witnessed the whole thing then said, "It looked like the rocking horse rocked a little bit when you picked the flashlight up."

"But I was not close enough to make the horse rock." I said.

"Yes, it was not you that made the rocking horse move and you definitely did not squeeze the horse's ear to make it go off either.

Both the lady and her boyfriend were ecstatic because they both knew what it was. Finally, someone else had seen the rocking horse go off for them. "No one believed us." they said.

"Well, I sure do. It startled me at first." I said. "What was better, we caught it on camera and even had someone watching the TV monitor while it happened. It pays to pay attention on these cases."

I noticed something was also blinking on the kid's bed. I realized what it was: the static box that I had set down. It's a good tool because it detects energy changes in the environment. If the energy fluctuates, the static box will flash on and off so it was clearly reading the energy difference then, which I was also feeling.

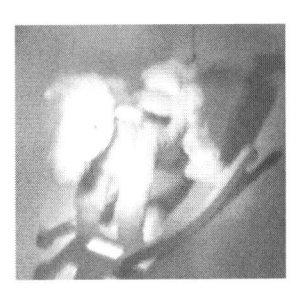

This is the rocking horse that was making sounds with no one touching it.

After going through my photos on my trail cam, I noticed something standing at the end of the hall, looking at us.

If you look at the lower, left-hand corner of this photo, you can see a figure standing there. The spirit seems very short from our vantage point. As we look at the doorway where the spirit is standing, we cannot tell if it was a child spirit or not, but I will let you form your own opinion. It seems to be about three to four feet tall. After looking at the history of this home we found out an older lady had died in this house.

THE EVIL ENTITY

A psychic medium who I work with a lot asked me if I could help her with a case. She mentioned that the woman she had spoken with said that she felt very unsafe in her home and needed help right away. "This is not your normal investigation, and I get a very strange feeling about it." the medium said.

I didn't like how she said "strange." It meant something bad to me because I'd never heard her discuss a case in this way before. However, I agreed to investigate with her help to assist her client with the house.

I was told that the home owners, the client and her husband, were so frightened that they had their local priest do a house blessing to help remove what they thought was "an evil entity in their home." I also found out that the home owners were really religious: The paranormal including ghosts went against their own belief systems. They actually cancelled appointments with us twice because they were conflicted about what they believed and whether or not to have paranormal investigators come to their home. However, after the house blessing with the priest didn't work, they figured they had to do something about the ghostly activity. We were their last chance to rid their home of what they thought was evil.

When we first arrived at the home, it did not feel too bad. I started walking through doing a baseline EMF or energy reading. I was shocked to see that it read "zero" in almost every room of the house. However, two rooms felt heavy. The first bedroom felt so heavy that it was hard to breathe in. It was almost suffocating to be in there. The woman walked over to me and said, "That's my father's bedroom. That's where a lot of the activity happens. We've seen dark shadows from that corner of the room. The evil shadow people crawl across the ceiling and down by his bed at night. He is very old, and it seems to bother him the most." She seemed scared just talking about it. "He wakes up with bruises and other weird marks on him."

"Well, hopefully we can fix that," I said, trying to give them some comfort in the knowledge that we were there to help them. The medium walked into the room. "Wow! It's heavy in here and you have a lot of spirits. One in particular one is staying back and not letting me get close to him. Did you walk in the bathroom yet? It's even heavier in there."

As I walked over to the bathroom, the air was so dense and thick that it was hard to even think or focus on what might be there. "Whew! I don't like the feeling in there either and the pressure I felt was very intense and not good."

I knew this investigation was going to be different, just like the medium had predicted. I figured that I had better get some equipment set up and get started. I thought I would try out my ghost box and see if we could get some spirit communication going.

The box started talking right as soon as I flipped the switch. The first words were "Jesus" and "Human" repeated several times. These kind of described the homeowners because they were very religious. The next word was "mommy" and then "paranormal" and "observe." These words from our ghost kind of explained what we were doing, too. The ghost later said "Emma" through the box. This is what the medium picked up as well. She said, "There is a little girl named Emma here. I just heard her say that she said her name is Emma."

I thought that was pretty good as the two connected. I got out my dowsing rods, which indicated that the energy was very strong there. With my dowsing swaying quickly back and forth I knew right away that I was picking up a child's energy.

It was the little girl we also got on the ghost box named Emma. All of a sudden, the dowsing rods slowed down, meaning that another spirit was coming through them. It was a strange feeling and seemed negative.

As the owners asked questions, the dowsing rods wouldn't answer. They completely stopped working, which usually never happens. "Wow! They do not like these questions or that we are figuring them out." the medium said. Then to the ghost she said, "That's okay 'cause you will be gone soon and you cannot harm these people again. I will make you leave." Just then, the dowsing rods started moving in the "yes" position.

"Interesting." I said. "Now they are working?" At that point, I was getting pretty drained, so I started to check my equipment. Almost every piece was drained too. Two of my recorders were flashing "low battery", so I took them out in the kitchen to replace them.

All of a sudden, I heard "Peter!" whispered near my ear. I looked around, but saw that no one was out in the kitchen near me so I went back to replacing the batteries.

Again, but louder this time, I heard my name called. There was no ghost box playing and it was quiet. I called out to the bedroom area where everyone was sitting, "Hey, did you guys call my name out? I just heard my name twice. The second one was really loud."

"No. We were in here just relaxing and being quiet."

So I asked again, "Really? You didn't just call out my name a minute ago?" I kind of knew this wasn't the case because the whispered voice was very close to me, but I felt I should verify it nonetheless. "Wow! That's nuts 'cause I heard it called twice just now." I said.

The medium said, "The spirit called your name, we didn't." When the medium verified this, I was a little distracted, wondering why they would call my name. This case was getting strange, just as the medium had said it was before we began to investigate.

"I'm getting drawn into the man's bedroom here, so I'm going to sit on the bed for a minute. Can you come down here with me and stand near the bedroom?" the psychic called.

"Sure," I called back. "I'll be right down."

All of a sudden, I heard, "Ouch! ...Shit!" The medium swiftly left the bedroom, looking at her finger. "Man, that hurts." she said. She walked down to the kitchen towards me. I noticed a huge, red mark on her finger. "Holy shit! That just happened?" I asked.

"Yeah, I was sitting on the bed when I suddenly had this burning sensation on my finger."

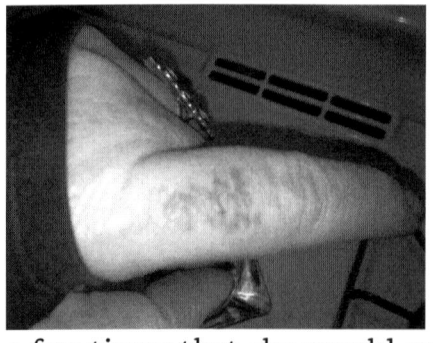

I grabbed my camera and snapped some photos of her hand. The medium ran some cold water on her finger. It was very red and bleeding in one spot. I could not believe what had just happened to her.

The medium mentioned a few times that she would get rid of the one spirit that was hiding on her if the entities present didn't tell her who it was. I think the wound was the spirits' way of getting back at her. Then I started thinking, "What if it's an inhuman entity and not a spirit at all?"

I went back to the ghost box, which was saying Human several times. Was that the one spirit who would not talk through my dowsing rods? This was getting interesting, so I walked down to the room the medium had just been harmed in. I wanted the spirit there to know that I was not scared of it and able to confront it. I had my dowsing rods out. The first question was, "Were you never born?"

The answer was, "No!"

"Are you the one harming these people living here?"

"Yes!"

"Do you know that the medium can get rid of you?"

"Yes!"

"Is that why you harmed her?"

"Yes!"

"I think we got enough information." the medium said. "We need to cleanse this house and just rid of this thing!"

I agreed. Whatever was there had to go because we'd all had enough happen to us by that time. The medium started smudging with many different sage bundles. I sprayed some of my special holy water mix and dowsed myself pretty well with it, too. I did not want anything negative attaching itself to me or following me home.

After the medium finished the cleansing, we could feel the difference there. Another crazy case was over with. "Hopefully, it will be calm again and these people can have some peace in their home." I thought.

At the end of the smudging ritual and just before we left, I asked the homeowners if they thought we did a good job. They told us that they liked how we had investigated the house. "Well, at first we didn't know what to expect and were terrified of having someone come to our home. But after seeing you work and how you helped, we will tell everyone about you guys and how great you are." they said.

"Actually, I have another investigation for you guys. Our friends have been having problems with their house, too." the psychic's client said.

I was happy we'd helped these very religious people and that they were happy with us. We actually did pick up another case from doing this one. This happens quite a lot as word of mouth is the best way to get more investigations. I like to follow up on cases, enjoying the input from the homeowners that we've investigated for. It makes us better as we gain more information and more experience working with people on paranormal investigations.

THE CASE OF POSSESSION

I received an e-mail from a lady who seemed pretty stressed-out about her home. "There is a lot going on here, and I need you to help me figure out what is here." she said.

I asked her what kind of activity was going on there and if she had more information she could share with me about the house.

"There is so much weird stuff going on here that we actually want to move out, but we can't afford it." she said. "I'm not working right now and have a lot of issues going on with me."

I wondered right away if her issues were connected to the house and if the spirits could be affecting her situation in some way. When I asked her what the past history of the house was, there was a long pause.

"Well, the past owner practiced Voodoo in the house. He was slaughtering goats and things like that. We also found some weird animal skulls and dark colored candles here when we moved in. Whatever the ghost is, it seems to be constantly tormenting me. It does not like me at all. I feel the energy here and it's not good. I can't sleep at night because I feel this being pulling my hair in a creepy kind of way. It's not a gentle pull. It's really forceful enough to pull my head off my pillow at night. I really don't sleep well here. We've all seen shadows moving around the house, mostly on the stairs, going up or down. It feels like they watch us, whatever we are doing. We never go down into the basement alone. It's way too creepy down there. If we do, it's a quick trip down and we practically run back up the stairs! We hear so many creepy noises that we cannot explain them all."

"Well, I will stop by and do a walk-through to see what kind of set up we will need. I also want to feel out the house to see what kind of energy is there. Some houses you can sense dark energy around." She felt relieved that I was planning to come over with the crew.

When I got there, she and her family started telling us what had happened in the kitchen. They said that they thought the spirits had been trying to kill them, given what the spirits had done in the house. "Like what?" I asked.

The lady of the house walked over to the stove area and showed me how a pizza box had been left on top of the stove. "But what scared us the most was what happened when we got home. We found that the pizza boxes had been burned down to ashes."

"Wow!"

"Yeah, and the stove was off. We weren't home and we didn't leave the pizza boxes there on the stove when we left. We would never do that! It's too dangerous."

"Most people would agree with that." one of my team members said.

"Well anyway, when we got home, the stove was off, but something turned on the burners 'cause the pizza boxes had burned up. When I checked the handles on the stove, they turned fairly hard. Someone would have to crank on them to get them to turn on. I checked the stove and the burners. Everything looked fine. Oh, and that's not all. We left a can of soup on top of one of the burners. The burner was off, but something turned that burner on. When the burner was turned on and the flame heated the can up, the can exploded and the contents hit the ceiling up there. You can still see the stain." She pointed to the spot on the ceiling. "We had a hard time cleaning it off."

I could not figure out or debunk any of these stories and our clients seemed pretty scared and tense when they were telling them. "A couple of times, the pilot lights were blown-out. We smelled the gas in the kitchen. The thing is no doors were opened and there was no wind, so we don't know how they were blown out."

The walked into the living room and pointed to a remote control car. "That was going around by itself last night." the husband said.

"You mean the remote control car?" I asked.

"Yes, and we thought the kids were playing around with the remote. But we checked, and the kids were upstairs sleeping. We found the remote on top of the counter. After the car stopped moving, we asked for the spirits to move the car forward, and it did. It's very creepy that the spirits could do that. Another time it was moving by itself and we had taken the batteries out of the remote control."

As we walked upstairs with them, they pointed at a pair of child monitors. "We had to unplug them and take them down. We were hearing strange noises on them, but the sounds were not from our kids. One night when they weren't even home, we heard small child talking on the baby monitor. Also our kids talk to the ghosts here, carrying on full conversations. It's pretty freaky when we hear them talking to invisible people. They say, 'Oh, they just want to play with us,' but there were so many noises on the baby monitors that we couldn't take it anymore, which is why we unplugged them. We had babysitters quit because they would see the shadow people moving around the house. One babysitter had her pant leg and shirt sleeve tugged on very hard when she was down in the living room. The kids were upstairs sleeping. It scared the crap out of her. She called us and told us we needed to come home right away. We also found a very old head stone in the backyard. We think the previous owners stole it and put it out back in the yard here. We had it removed and taken back to the nearby cemetery. The neighbors knew the previous owner who lived here and said, 'He practiced dark magic in the house. He purchased a goat every month and would use them as sacrifices.'"

"Whoa! Pretty creepy," I said.

"Yes, and there are still goat legs down in the basement."

"What? They are still down there?"

The lady continued, "Yes. We just found them a little while back. Whatever is here, it drains my energy. I can barely move around now because I'm totally drained while I'm in my house. My back is killing me and I can't even function, let alone go to work this way. Oh, every owner who has lived here in this house has died of cancer, or so I'm told. This really makes us nervous. We don't want to get cancer or have any illnesses. Everyone knows this house is haunted, and some even say it's cursed. On Halloween, we played with an Ouija board and things got even worse. That night, we were drinking and my husband…" she paused. "Well, he was like, possessed!"

"What do you mean possessed? Was he acting weird? What happened?" I asked.

"Later that night, he started acting really weird. His eyes were not right. He went crazy; running after me and my girlfriend. We started to fight him off because it seemed like he wanted to attack us. It was not him at all. He was acting like a lunatic. I squared-off and kicked him straight in the groin area, but he never flinched. I know any other man would have fallen over on the floor, but he did not even flinch. Nothing! Finally, a bunch of us held him down until he calmed. He does not remember any of it. It scared the hell out of us!"

"Do you still have the Ouija board here?"

"We did not know what to do with it so yes! It's in the attic. We covered it with a Jesus cloth."

"If the Ouija board is open it could be the portal in your house now by giving the spirits a way to enter into your home and adding to the activity here."

"The activity did seem to worsen after that. I don't play around with it now." she admitted in an almost apologetic way.

Her statement made me wonder if she was telling to tell the truth. She seemed to be covering that part up for some reason. "Can I go down to the basement?" I asked.

"Yes, you can, but I will stay up here. I hate going anywhere near the basement." she said. "Maybe if you go down in the basement I might go halfway down the stairway."

I quickly made my way down the steps. It did feel creepy down there. I found the goat legs she was referring to along with some old bottles. One bottle had a creepy, fuzzy thing inside it. "God knows what's in these old bottles." I said to myself.

The lady walked partially down the stairs toward me when something started to spike my EMF meter that I had in my hand. "That's weird." I said. "It's almost like you set my EMF meter off."

Another investigator noticed the same thing. She quickly ran back up the stairs. "That is creepy." she said. "I hope it's not following me or attached to me somehow."

I started to wonder then if it could be a spirit attachment. Usually spirits have the ability to latch onto some people who are very open to the spirit world. When she told me she was three quarters Native American, it made me wonder. Native American people are usually very sensitive and open to different energies, from what I have seen. As I looked around upstairs I noticed two kids playing in their rooms who I did not realize were in the house. One of the kids looked at me and said, "I hear knocking on my outside window at night. It scares me because I don't know who is knocking on my window. It might be the man that I've seen here." he said.

"I don't like the old man I see here sometimes because he is scary!" the little girl said.

"Yes, they scare me a lot. I don't like them when they scare me."

"Sounds like we will have to figure out what's going on here." I said. I told the owners I never investigate while kids are in the home so we made plans so she could have the kids stay overnight at another house while we were investigating the home.

When we arrived back at the house a week later, we could still feel the energy there. It felt as if the spirits were watching every move we made there. We quickly wired-up the house with night vision cameras and static lights as well as EMFs detectors laid out. We set many trigger objects out, too.

The lady brought over a stuffed bear that would start clapping and making noise if the spirits set it off. "Here," she said, "this toy has gone off by itself many times. I think the spirit kids like this toy and mess around with it." I checked it out and could not set the toy off without touching it.

"Okay. I will put the toy in front where my camera will catch it if it does go off." I said.

We were just finishing up when my brother said, "What are you doing with the night vision camera upstairs now?"

"Ah, nothing. I'm right here next to you in the hallway." I said.

"Well, who the hell is moving the camera up in the air right now?" he said.

"No one is up there as I accounted for everyone that was there."

All of a sudden, we heard a loud crash! "Yep, your camera just went flying off the cabinet. I saw it here on the video monitor." No one was around the camera as it just rose up into the air and flew across the room! I heard a loud noise, so I rushed upstairs with them behind me.

"Yep, here is the camera lying on the floor, but how did it get way over here?" I asked.

"I was watching the TV monitor: the camera just rose up and sailed across the room." he said.

"This is crazy! Was it recording then?"

"No, not at that moment. The cameras were powered up and working and I was just getting ready to push the record button on when it happened."

"I could see that no one was up there." he said. "Well, it was good you were watching the monitors." I said.

"Well, I'd accounted for everyone I know and I could see that no one was up there, too."

"We haven't even started investigating yet, but things are already flying off the shelf." I said.

"Yeah. That's my bedroom where it happened, too." the lady said. She was a little freaked out by what had just happened. I could not blame her. I could not figure out how my camera had been thrown off the stand either, so I set the camera back up and this time, duct taped it down to the stand. "There. It will have to rip the duct tape in order to move the camera now." I said.

We started our investigation and right away, began getting many EMF hits and hearing weird noises. All of a sudden, I heard a tearing sound and a loud thud noise again. "What the hell? Not again!" I said.

"Yep, your camera is on the floor again." The investigator said.

"'Can't be," I said. "I duct taped it down to the stand; there is no way that's possible." Sure enough, when I walked into the room, the camera had been thrown onto the floor. But this time, it wasn't working. The picture was fuzzy and the camera was broken and split apart at the base of it. And now there was no sound on it. "Great! Now it's breaking stuff." I said. I got another camera out, but this time, I put it lower on the tripod.

As we watched the cameras down in the basement, I noticed my motion lights were being set off by something. So, we went down there to check them out. We started getting very high energy hits on our EMF meters. "Well, something is down here." I said. The static lights were also going off near the goat legs in the basement. "Seems like we are getting many hits on different pieces of equipment." the owner said.

"Oh, there is an attic upstairs, too." she told me. I instantly wanted to go up there.

"I want to go up there." I said.

"Well, it has a really small access hole to it."

"Not a problem," I said, "I will squeeze through it." When I got through the hole and started looking around, I noticed a very old makeshift block on the floor. It appeared that someone was using it to chop things up as there was many hack marks on top of it. It looked like it was charred, too. "Holy shit! I wonder if this is what they were chopping up the goats with," I said. "It needs to go as I don't like the energy it holds."

It felt creepy up there. I had to tear some of the box apart to get it through the hole. I noticed another box with ashes in it. It looked very old. "I wonder what in the Hell is in those ashes?" I said. I took the box downstairs to see what it was. "This is not good; better take all this stuff outside."

I had the feeling it was not helping with the energy in the home. I gathered up all the things from the basement and took them outside. I discarded the goat legs and old bottles; anything that seemed like it did not belong in the house. At one point, the owner said, "Over there! I just saw a shadow go through that room over there." There was no camera in the small room.

"That's usually how it happens: There is no camera to catch it." I said.

At one point, I heard a noise upstairs. "What is that noise?" I asked.

"Oh, that's the stuffed bear that claps his hands and makes noises. It's going off now." the lady of the house said. I walked over to the TV monitors. Sure enough, the bear was talking and making noises by itself. Everyone was accounted for, and in order for the bear to work, someone would have had to squeeze the bear's paw to activate it. "Well, no one is touching that bear." the lady of the house said.

"Well, not that we can see, human-wise." one of our investigators said.

"But something is making that bear go off." I said. While we were running the ghost box, we had several messages come through it. They were not good messages, either. It said, "Fuck you!" and "Get out!" I did not like the profanity from the box, whatever was there just wanted us out.

After a while, the house seemed to calm down. It was getting late, so we packed it up. Everyone seemed drained and ready to leave. The next week, while I was going through the video, I plainly saw the bear operating by itself and my camera flying off the shelf without assistance. I knew I needed a psychic medium to go to the house and see if she could get rid of the negative source which was probably causing the activity there.

When the medium arrived at the house, she quickly picked up on several things. "One spirit does not like the lady of the house. She does not clean the house enough like used to back in the day. The spirit watches over the children and she likes them here. I'm also getting her husband. I think he practiced dark magic here, or something very ritualistic." She paused briefly to check on something we could not see. "Oh, yeah: He was into black magic here. He was scared of what was here in the house." the medium said. "This house had been haunted way before this guy was here. They say he slept with a loaded gun with him because he was scared of all the weird things and noises at night. He used the dark magic to try to protect himself from the spirits here. Something happened out back on this land." She walked towards the back yard. "Yes, a woman was murdered out back here years ago. Out there by that row of trees." she pointed. "Oh, and the neighbors heard a lady screaming in the middle of the night. That's where they heard her screaming back by the woods."

The medium walked back into the house. "I'm getting spirit children here, too. You have many spirits here. Who was playing with the Ouija board?" the medium said. "It's upstairs, isn't it? I feel it upstairs. Go and get the board now." she said firmly.

The girl walked down with the board. "Oh, my God! That board is open and allowing spirits to enter through it." She quickly walked it outside and tossed the board to the ground. "I feel the air rushing out of the board." she said. I reached my hands down by the board and sure enough, I could feel cold air rushing from out from the board. "Wow, it's 80 degrees out here, but it feels like 40 degrees by that board." There was extremely cold air coming out. "Well, I will close it so nothing more can come through the board." the medium said.

After the medium finished clearing the board, the owner walked back inside. "Did you see that?" the medium asked.

"What?"

"Her eyes! They turned black twice!"

"Holy shit! Really?" I asked.

"Yep. We are not through yet. We need to find out who is in there with her tonight. I'm going to have to put her under hypnosis and remove the attachment." she said.

"Can you do that?"

"Yes, but it's going to take some work to remove whoever is attached to her, though."

We had the lady sit down in a chair. The medium, who was also a certified hypnotherapist, soon said she was deep under hypnosis. The medium started asking the lady questions. First, she asked what her name was. "I don't know." the lady said.

"Who are you?"

"I don't know." the lady said.

The medium looked at me and said in a low voice, "This going to take some work. It is not letting her speak."

"I want to talk to whoever is in there with this girl! I command you to tell me your name!" she said firmly to the lady.

"Nicole…" the lady said slowly.

The medium looked at me and said, "That's not her name." At this point, I did not tell the medium anything about this case so we could confirm that she had gotten all of the information by using her psychic abilities.

"No, that's not her name." I confirmed. She seemed to be getting more agitated as we gained more information about what was there with her. And at that moment, we suddenly had another piece of the puzzle: her name.

I found myself thinking that the girl was going to jump out of the chair and start choking the shit out of us. I guess I have watched too many movies where exorcisms were performed. That's what usually happens: The possessed person jumps out of the bed or chair and goes after the exorcist with a vengeance. Needless to say, I was a little nervous by then.

The medium held the girl and looked directly into her eyes. "You need to leave NOW!" She shouted at her. "You cannot stay with her!"

All of a sudden, I heard knocking on the front door. "Don't answer that; it's trying to throw us off." she said. It was a very loud knocking noise. I peeked outside and noticed that no one was on the front porch. It was very creepy, to say at the least. The medium yelled again, "I command you to leave her now! You cannot stay there with her."

The lady was mumbling, "No, no." It was very unnerving. Finally, things seemed to calm down.

Suddenly, the back door swung open by itself right behind me! "Holy shit! Did you see that?" I asked.

"Yes, I think it just left the house." the medium said.

"It?" I said. "This has been a crazy night. Do you think she is okay now?" I asked.

"Yes. I need to take her out of the sleep and see how she feels now. "But before that I will ask her what her real name is and see if she gives me the right name. The medium asks the girl, and she replies back the right answer. "Ha, that's good. It's gone and we can wake her up now."

As the girl slowly wakes up I can see her facial expressions seemed calmer and less agitated. "How do you feel now?" the medium asked.

"Wow! I feel great and my back doesn't hurt now. What happened?"

"Well, the back pain was not your back pain. There was something attached to you." she said. I got rid of it and you should feel better now."

"I feel better already." the lady said. The whole house felt lighter including the air. As we walked outside, the dogs were lined up and just staring at us. "Look!" The medium said, "The animals cannot believe we got rid of those spirits. They would thank me if they could talk."

"The dogs do seem to be standing in a line; staring at us like you did it!" It was funny, except when the medium looked down into the ashes of the old box I had brought outside.

"There are teeth and bones in there." she said. "They were burning things in it. It's good that you got that out of there because the old goat leg has dark energy attached to it. You were right to get them out the house."

"God, I'm glad we are finished! This whole case was creepy." I said.

"Yes, the bad energy here needed to go. But, it's gone now and things should get better here." I just shook my head.

The owners said, "Thank you. We will let you know how things will turn out." The owners later reported a lot less activity and the lady returned to work with no other issues. We were glad to help them out, but I was glad this case was resolved and over with.

The medium could see the dark energy around the old goat leg so she suggested taking a picture, and it shows up on this photo. If you look closely, you can see a dark ring around my arm by my elbow to my hand area.

BLACK ANGEL OF DEATH

This story was interesting to me, so I thought to share it with you:

A lady called me about some very strange activity in her home. She said, "I don't know why, but I'm seeing full figures in my house."

"Oh, full body apparitions?" I asked.

"Yes, but they are scary." the lady said. "I live in an old farm house by myself and I sleep upstairs on the second floor. One night, I was startled by a noise coming from next to my bed. I looked over and saw an older man, kneeling down on the floor. The man was going through my purse and pulling items out of it. I thought, 'Oh my God! I'm getting robbed!' and reached for my cell phone. But as did so, I looked closer at the man and noticed that the man's right shoulder was see-through. At that point I knew then the man was not real and that he must be a ghost! As I was looking at the ghost man, he must have realized I could see him because he slowed his movements and looked right up at me. When this man made eye contact. He made *the nastiest* and most evil-looking face at me, then the ghost man vaporized right in front of me. I was shaking so bad." the lady said.

Then, she took a breath and continued, "I could not believe what I'd just witnessed. About a week later, I had another visit. This time, it was not the man though. It was very late and I had been woken up by the sound of metal clanking around. I looked over towards my jewelry box (that's where the sound was coming from) and noticed a little girl standing by it. She was playing with my jewelry and giggling. As I watched the little girl, she suddenly looked my way and noticed that I could see her. She got extremely nervous and put the jewelry back. Then she quickly vanished. I wasn't afraid of the little girl, though.

Next is what scared me the most though. Just thinking about it makes me shiver and I get goose bumps every time I talk about it. One night, I noticed some movement over by my window. I could plainly see whatever it was coming in through it. My window is very high off the ground and that night, it was also closed, so I knew it was not a solid person. Whatever it was came in and stood close to my bed. It appeared to be an angel, but something was wrong: It was totally black! All of sudden, it started to open up something behind its back. It had what looked like wings on its back. The wings opened up further and I knew this was not good." The lady told me that she got a very bad feeling that whatever was going to happen that she knew it would not be good.

A week later she found out that a very close relative had died. "I can't help but think that this black angel had something to do with it." she said. I have heard of the black angel of death before. People say it can mean someone will die or it's a sign of death and someone will die soon if you see one. By listening to this lady I do know that she seemed gifted and it may have been a sign to her that something bad was going to happen. I just hope I never see a black angel of death. It must have been unnerving for the lady to see something like that.

I never investigated the black angel of death house, but think this lady was somehow very gifted and could see ghosts. I explained this to her and she seemed to agree with me, saying that the psychic gift ran in the family. This was however a very intense story and one I will never forget.

HOSPICE / AFTERLIFE

My own personal story took place when my father's health was failing and I was spending my last days with him. When my father was alive, he always said, "This afterlife stuff is a bunch of hocus pocus crap," and he did not believe in ghosts. Even though he had seen an angel sitting on a fence post at the same time that one of his family members had passed away. He always had an explanation for what had happened to him. He said he must have imagined it somehow.

As my father grew weaker and more ill, he began to tell me things that startled me. I sat with him in the hospital as he was gazing behind me. Suddenly, he said, "Hey! What are all these people doing here in the room with us?" At the time, I was the only person in the room. So it threw me off and made me think, "What is he seeing and why is he seeing people that are not here?" I questioned this because my dad was a skeptic all of his life and I could not figure out why he was seeing people who were not there. I asked him, "Who are these people with us?" He mentioned some old war buddies from a long time ago.

When my mom walked in the room with us, I asked her, "Who is this person that Dad has just mentioned? He said his name was Bud."

"Oh, he was an old war soldier who was in the army with your father." she explained.

I said, "Oh, what is he up to now?"

"Well, he died while serving, and he's no longer alive. In fact, he hasn't been alive for many years. Why?"

"Well, Dad just mentioned he'd just seen this guy from the war in his hospital room."

"That's impossible." she said.

"Well, he acted like he had a conversation with him and almost like he was in the room with us. It was startling, to say the least. Why is my dad seeing old, dead, war buddies?" I asked. We were very puzzled.

The next night, my dad looked up at the ceiling and yelled, "Not NOW!" then, "NO!" We looked over to see who he was talking to, but there was no one in the room with us at the time. "No, I'm not ready. Leave me alone!" he yelled. I scratched my head.

"Who is he talking to?" I asked. Again, we had no clue what was happening.

I grabbed some literature off of the hospice stand. It said that we might have experiences like this as our loved ones got closer to death. I was shocked to see what it said in writing. I thought, "Really? This must happen a lot. It's actually in print and very common when someone gets closer to death."

We did not want dad to stay in the hospital any longer so we had him transferred home so he could be around family and friends. I did not think of him leaving us and dying. It was nice to know people were waiting for my father on the other side and that he didn't have to be alone when he did cross over. What was happening at the time never quite registered though. It really made me think about people crossing over and the Afterlife. It was just another reason that made me wonder about the Afterlife. Death will do that to you. It really does make you think about it. It is also another reason which pushed me into paranormal investigations. I wanted to answer some of my own questions about the Afterlife like why did my own dad, being a skeptic all his life, start seeing dead people. Were they waiting just on the Other Side? Maybe there was a thin realm that we did not know about or see? Why did his spiritual views change as he got more ill? Was he growing more spiritual as he got closer to death? Why did the hospice literature actually say that some people might see dead relatives as they grew sicker?

There were so many questions I had going through my mind. (Just for the record, I think the hospice program is the best that anyone can ask for. They give peace to a family member or friend passing away at home with family around them.) I worried about seeing my dad pass on, and wondered if I would always be affected by it.

It was sad to see him leave, but when he did pass on it was almost a peaceful feeling. There was almost a peaceful energy in the room.

This is my own assessment of this passing. I know some people will not agree with me. It was just a feeling that I got that he would be okay on the other side. I still grieve and wonder why he had to go so soon. It did not matter what age they are. They are gone forever, so you can never see them again. One thing that will stay with me is when my dad said he would never change a thing about his life and was happy the way he lived it. I hope I can say that before I pass on. My mom mentioned the story about getting pennies from Heaven and maybe that would happen.

It was not long after my dad passed that we started seeing pennies everywhere. My mom especially was finding pennies in very weird places. She would find a penny on the phone receiver right after she was on the phone and on top of things she had just set down. She would turn around to find a penny there. Soon, my mom had a mason jar full of pennies from my dad.

The day after my dad passed, I had laid down to try to catch up on some sleep. I checked the alarm clock. Then, I turned over to get some shut eye. The next thing I heard was a few pennies rolling off of the night stand. "That's weird." I said to myself because I'd just checked the alarm clock and knew there were no pennies there before that. Then, more pennies starting rolling off the stand! "What is going on?" I asked myself, "And why are there a half dozen pennies just coming from nowhere and rolling off the night stand?" It was so bazar that even today, I can't believe that this happened to me. I like to rationalize why things happen so there is no way I could explain this or how it was even possible. However, I feel that my dad was trying to tell me that he was still around me and at peace.

I also got weird calls to my phone. There were actually phone messages left by a man who had a very low voice and was very hard to hear. I instantly thought of my dad. I'm not sure why I felt that. When I checked for a phone number to see who was trying to call me, there was no ID number on the phone. We had the ID caller set up on our phone, so the number always comes up when someone calls us. It was another strange event I could not explain, so it has always stuck with me to this day. I'm still thinking about it.

Three weeks later, someone asked how my dad was doing. "Oh, didn't you hear? He passed away a few weeks ago." The guy just looked at me like, "What? I'm sure I saw your dad, walking around his house a week ago! He always wears that blue coat." he said.

I said, "Yes. He had a blue coat that he wore a lot."

"Yup, that's what he was wearing, and I'm sure it was your dad walking around his house just last week." The guy's face was almost white, like he had seen a ghost. "Well, who knows? Maybe he did."

These events propelled us into thinking more about the afterlife. I was even more than curious as a result of what had happened to me. So, I wanted to know more about the afterlife, and to start doing paranormal investigations.

I must add the small experience that happened after all

this: I had visited a place called Lily Dale in NY. This is a spiritual camp where psychics reside. I went to a group reading by a place called the Spiritual Tree. There were at least fifty people in the group when the medium looked up at me. "You! In the red shirt, standing at the back area, there," she called to me. "The book you just purchased…" she continued.

"Yes? What about that book?" I asked.

"You will be doing the same thing in less than a year from now."

The book I'd just purchased was about ghost investigations. I was stunned and could not figure out how she knew that. I'd purchased the book back in the store before I had even gotten to Lily Dale. It was still in the plastic bag with the receipt inside the book. I think I stated, "I don't think so. I don't even have equipment or a website."

"You will be doing that type of work." she insisted. "Just remember that."

Guess what? In less than a year later, I had a website, ghost hunting equipment, and paranormal investigations in peoples' houses. Who would have thought?

VISITATIONS

Probably one of the most common things I've heard from many people is that they've experienced visitations after a loved one has passed on. Knowing what I do, they usually want to tell me their stories. After all, most people would think that they were crazy after hearing their stories because they've bought into the idea that people who see things like ghosts must be losing their minds or they just write it off as being tired, but many people have told me they have had visits from their loved ones after they had passed on.

Most of these stories are not scary. Usually, the spirits are just loved ones trying to say, "Hey, it's okay. I have moved on." They usually contact with their relatives or friends within a short time of their passing. It is not that the spirits are trying to scare them. They are attempting to let them know that they are okay and that their living loved ones don't have to worry about them. Although it can be hard for some people to see their loved ones after they have died, most people say that it was not scary. Some even felt better after seeing them and a few people even received messages from the spirits. One lady said, "I could clearly see my grandma standing by my bed. I noticed she was trying to say something to me. I did not hear the words, but I could tell she was saying, 'I love you' and 'don't worry about me.'"

It was very comforting for this lady to interact with her late grandma. She started to feel a sense of closure and peace knowing she had just received this special message from her grandma. Some people say that it's in their minds, that they are mentally conjuring up the spirits to make themselves feel better. However, most people tell me they know they were not sleeping and actually sitting up in bed and could clearly see their past loved ones communicating with them.

Some of our local lectures bring in spirits. In one lecture at a community college, I had my dowsing rods out while explaining how they could detect and pick up energy around people. The students asked if they had energy around them and if they could dowse in the classroom. I said, "Okay, but I can't control where they'll point or who could come through at this time."

When I started dowsing, the rods quickly pointed to a guy in the back row. "Whoa! Why are they pointing at me?" he said.

"Well, there is energy around you and I don't think it's bad." I said. I asked if he had anyone pass on whom he knew. The rods quickly crossed for "yes."

"They just said yes?" the guy asked.

"Yep," I said. I asked my rods if it was a male energy and I got another quick cross for "yes."

"Oh! I know who it is if it's a male." the boy said. He looked at my dowsing rods and asked if it was his grandfather who was around him. My rods quickly moved for a big "yes." I could feel the energy around me as the hair on my arms stood up.

"Yep. I feel him now." I said.

The boy said, "Wow! That's so cool because me and grandfather were really close and I miss him."

The rods quickly acknowledged that the boy was talking. "I think he just watches over you and probably protects you in a way." I said.

The rods crossed for "yes" again. The boy's eyes gleamed with extreme happiness with the knowledge that his grandfather was around him and watching over him. The teacher nodded over at me to almost say, "Yep. You got it." What all of the college students did not know was that the teacher was a clairvoyant who could see ghosts, too.

After the class was over, a few college students followed us out, still talking about some of their own experiences. These were the ones that they did not want to disclose in front of the whole class. It was cool to connect with some of the students because they were clearly relieved to be able to discuss the paranormal experiences they had been keeping to themselves for quite a while.

At the end of the second seminar, I looked over at the teacher and asked her what she'd seen in the classroom. "I know that look: you caught something." I said.

"Yes. I wanted to say something to the boy, but being a teacher in a high profile position, I could not say anything to him. I will tell you, though, because everyone has left the classroom. When you were dowsing around the boy, I could see his grandfather standing right behind him with his outstretched hands on his shoulders." she said.

"Wow! That's so cool because I always wonder if my rods are right about who is there."

"Oh, yeah." she nodded in agreement. "His grandfather was right behind him and seemed happy that you were making a connection between him and his grandson."

I'm always amazed by how these experiences happen and I don't write them off as just coincidences. They happen for a reason, and I knew that talking to these kids was actually helping them. Children need someone to share their beliefs and not judge them in any way. They need to hear from loved ones who have passed on or someone else who is dead to actually believe in their own paranormal experiences. I truly know that these paranormal experiences are real for these kids by witnessing their faces light up as connections are made and the stories are told.

    I have also made many friends and have met so many people who I shared not only frightening experiences with, but think I have helped in some way or another. Ghost hunting is priceless, so I can never complain about the countless hours I have put into the field. I know it was meant for me to get into this field and help so many people out. I believe we are drawn into certain positions to help people, too. Many psychic mediums tell me that our souls are charted in advance and the way to travel through life is already planned and that this is why we are drawn to certain people or jobs. I think there is a Force that connects us in certain ways. Some friends I have now are ones who I cannot remember meeting or under what conditions we had met. However, I do know that we crossed each other's paths for a reason and that our meeting was written into our charts as a learning experience during our time here on earth.

CROSSING OVER LOST SOULS

Through work in the paranormal field, I have witnessed many unexplained events. One part of what I do involves helping people in their homes to stop or decrease spirit activity or at least calm it down. What I did not realize initially was that not only living people, but spirits need help to find closure too. You can call it "lost souls" or "earthbound spirits." I know it sounds like a clip out of a movie, but it is true. When I go into an investigation, I look for different scenarios or similar events that might play out. Did the people lose someone close them? Was a possible suicide involved or was it someone connected to the house the owners live in now who is the ghost/causing the activity to happen?

There are many different ways a spirit will try to get noticed. Why are these people being bothered in their own home? It's important to investigate a home, but it is even more important to try to fix the house haunting. This is why this part is so important while doing investigations. Helping families find closure is probably the biggest way of helping.

Sometimes, it is not the living people who need closure. It's the departed soul who needs it. This is where it gets tricky, so I will explain it the best way I can.

Yes, getting evidence is one step while doing investigations. Taking the evidence and backing it up, with either actual historic events or family connections, is far more important. After I complete an investigation and find actual proof, I know that the family needs closure, or that they need help with what is going on in a home, so I usually bring in a psychic medium to help that family. I do this because I know that a good psychic medium can bring closure to a restless spirit and cross them over if needed. The ghost may be a confused spirit who still thinks he or she owns the home the people are having activity in. The client may have some psychic abilities of his or her own and needs help dealing with that gift, which is why the ghost is attracted to the house or trying to get a message across in the first place. Sometimes, the apparition is connected to a family member and there is a very important message that he or she needs to pass on. Only a very developed psychic medium can accurately speak with the dead and pass messages on to the living. The psychic must be able to really hear what is being said, and she or he has to be someone trustworthy.

When I return to a client's home with a psychic medium, I do not give any information about the case to the psychic. It's very important not to lead a psychic in any one direction. Therefore, I let her or him get the information and form conclusions without any help. Only if I think the deceased is dangerous or there is something really important about the case that the psychic needs to know will I tell him or her about it. I have worked with some amazing psychics and know that they are the real deal. In most of the cases I have worked on, the family members have gotten the closure they needed. The look on a person's face when the medium tells her or him something personal about a family member who has passed on or about what she or he is experiencing in a home is priceless. "How do you know that?" they usually ask the psychic.

The answer from the medium: "As a psychic medium I just know things. After all I am psychic."

I have seen spirit children that may have been drawn to the children in a home. In those cases, the spirit children are happy to find other children to play with and do not realize what might be happening there. The spirits usually do not realize that they are scaring the living kids in a home – or more often scaring the parents. When this happens, the psychic makes contact with the deceased children and explains that they cannot do this. Sometimes the psychic also assists the spirit children to move onto the Other Side or Heaven so they do not have to stay earthbound.

How does a medium move a spirit to the Light or Heaven? Some mediums tell me they can form a light and have the spirit move to the light and cross them over. Some mediums just communicate with the spirit and explain they are dead or tell them that they need to be with their family now. They move the spirit on by doing this. After witnessing many spirits cross over and feeling the peace after the heaviness has been lifted in a house, I've become aware that the mediums give the clients and spirits much needed closure. The family resumes their daily routine without further paranormal activity because the spirit they were dealing with is at rest now.

How do I know this? I usually do a follow up call or return to ask the family if they are experiencing any more activity. Most of the time, I can actually feel the difference before I even leave a home the same night the medium crosses the spirit over. The heavy pressure or feeling is lifted from the home when the spirit is brought to the Light. Sometimes, there will be some residual activity there in the home for a while, but then the activity ceases. Sometimes, I have had people tell me they actually missed the spirits being around them. They tell me, "You know, I miss that little girl spirit." or "I felt some connection to the spirit there and miss her playing with my stuff over here." They quickly say, "But it feels better here now and more peaceful." So, it's not only the living who need peace; it can be a spirit that needs peace as well.

Seeing what a good medium can do is amazing. Having a gift and using it to help so many people and spirits find peace is

PETER KANELLIS

amazing to me.

USEFUL TERMS EXPLAINED

Water is Energy

In my travels, I have often observed the surroundings of some of my paranormal investigations such as a nearby stream or some other kind of natural water supply. I do believe that water is a good energy source. Flowing water is especially powerful and has more appeal than stagnant or still water to spirits. Ghosts require a lot of energy to manifest or stir-up activity, so many times, my dowsing rods have pointed to the water as the spirits were taking the energy from it.

I didn't know why my dowsing rods would point to a stream or pull toward the water in the beginning, but I now understand what water does for the spirits. If there is a high amount of activity happening in a home, there may be water nearby, aiding them with its energy so they can manifest activity.

EVPs

EVP stands for "electronic voice phenomenon." This is a digital recorder that can hear ghostly voices and play them back. Usually, we cannot hear the spirit voices until the recorder is played back. So, the recordings provide concrete evidence that a spirit has made contact/ been present in a home or other location. It takes a lot of energy for a spirit to talk back to the questioner, so I usually ask a spirit questions while the recorder is on; pausing in-between questions to give the spirit time to answer them. It is always exciting to hear what is said.

EMFs

EMF stands for "electro-magnetic fields." EMF meters are used to locate the energy that a spirit can emit. It's important to rule-out natural/electrical energy sources such as radios, lamps, and clocks in a home, too. Although these appliances use electrical energy, they also store some of it. This energy can be detected with other devices.

We also do a sweep of a house or baseline EMF reading of the energy when we initially enter a client's home. EMFs can change, so the first reading is often different than the second and third. We use this information to get an average baseline EMF reading for a given house so we can tell the difference between that reading and the readings we get when there is psychic phenomena in the home.

Ley Lines

Ley lines were created thousands of years ago by man and natural forces through cracks and fissures in rock. These cracks seem to create the space for electromagnetic energy to gather. That energy follows the cracks up to the land surface and deep down into the ground. Some people think that the cracks or openings can help produce magnetic fields or vortexes from under homes where paranormal activity may be happening.

I have had people map out areas where we have investigated, and they have noted that many ley lines were indeed running under some of the homes with a lot of paranormal activity in them. Can we say for sure that it is true that ley lines have energy which can be the source of the activity? No, but it's another theory out there that should not be over looked or unnoticed.

Automatic Writing

Some psychic mediums can write out messages delivered to them from ghosts. The spirits will either dictate the message to the medium, who then writes it down or possess the medium's body to write out the messages themselves. The latter is called "automatic writing." The writing is messy sometimes, but that is because messages are usually written from the spirit guiding the medium's hand and some spirits just have messy handwriting. Messages from friendly ghosts are usually given because a client needs to hear what they have to say in order to affect a certain outcome. Spirits usually have issues that still need to be resolved, or can see that our clients have issues, so these messages can be critical to fixing problems.

Channeling

Some psychic mediums listen to the spirits talking to them and repeat the messages, or allow them to take over their bodies to deliver the messages themselves. The latter is what most people think of when they hear about channeling. Some clients can do this, but usually, it is performed by a trained psychic medium because there are risks involved. When the spirit jumps into the body, the medium can take on the spirit's personality. The medium says what the spirit wants to communicate to the people there in the home.

It can be easier for mediums to channel spirits who are outside of the mediums' bodies. It can be scary, though if the mediums lose control of what the spirits are doing. Ghosts have been known to try to take control of mediums' bodies for their own benefit and refuse to leave right away. The mediums have to be in control of what is happening when they are in contact with these entities.

Forms of Spirit Attachments

Attachments can happen in many different ways. I have seen attachments occur during Ouija Board sessions. Usually, the person is very open and the spirits will sense this and be drawn to the person. You can call them, "Hitchhikers," where a spirit sees a very open person and follows him or her home. An attachment can occur due to the person being so open. When I say, "Open," it can mean that this person is a very gifted psychic and/or very sensitive to spirits. Usually, he or she has no idea that this can occur until paranormal activity starts happening around them.

Another form of attachment can be caused by a very traumatic event that triggers said attachment. Some people say, "Well, it's a mental health issue and not paranormal at all." However, I have seen people go through a tragedy or event, after which they have seemed to have been imprinted with or attached to real energy. If they hold on to this form of energy and not let it go, it continues to manifest until it becomes a bigger issue.

Being empathic can also lead to energy which clings to a person. The empath is so open that he or she takes on another person's grief/emotions or spiritual energy. This can lead to a real attachment which needs to be removed.

Manifestations

Different kinds of paranormal phenomena can manifest and get out of control. These activities can center on a very religious person or someone who is fearful of the paranormal. He or she starts to have activity in the home and then reacts to the occurrences due to personal views. When this happens, he or she creates even more energy and gives a large amount of it to the spirit. Then all of a sudden, you have a large amount of kinetic or ghostly activity, and sometimes even poltergeist-type activity. This is because the person feeds the energy and makes it bigger than it had become from the fear it was originally fed.

Any type of strong emotion can trigger activity in a home. One person told me they were highly upset when they found out their daughter eloped with her boyfriend. When she walked through their restaurant, the pictures started to fly off the walls, and glasses were thrown around and off the tables. They manifested the activity there by the strong emotions they had been feeling. I have also seen this in homes where there were heated arguments in the house. The air came alive with activity. The people arguing actually fed the small amount of activity and created a huge problem there. One guy called me and blamed the spirits where they lived. He said, "She moved out yesterday and never called me back. We never had problems before until moving into this house. There is a dark presence here and it has been tearing us apart. I don't know where she is now. We fought and argued in this house and everything went very dark here after that."

I still wonder if they fed the energy and they actually caused most of the issues there. It's all in theory though after working on many cases and hearing many stories.

Theories

I have to talk about why I say, "It's all in theory," a lot. The word *paranormal* is based on something we cannot explain. Even after investigating many haunted areas and seeing what was happening at the time, I couldn't figure out or even rationalize much of it. I still cannot say I'm an expert in this field. I'm still learning, experimenting, and finding out that ghosts and related phenomena are really only based on theories and things we cannot explain. We will eventually find out when we cross over to the Other Side, and only then will we know for sure how our spirits will continue on even after death.

Sensitive People

As the paranormal field advances, we are finding many similar events that produce hauntings or paranormal activity. I feel that sensitive people do draw spirits to them as they can sense and feel spirits around them. One psychic medium explained to me that it almost seems spirits can sense that a person can see or feel them and it causes a "beacon of a light house" effect. I usually ask people if they think they are sensitive or have heightened senses that may be hyping up activity in a home. When I say sensitive that usually means that they have some form of psychic ability. Some people do not actually realize that they are sensitive, and it's up to me to explain why they are seeing spirits in their home or why only certain people can see them, but others cannot.

I have seen spirits connected with the owners who follow them from one place to another, only because they draw in spirits or can connect with them. I think almost everyone is psychic to some degree or in some sense. I have even seen some people visit a doctor to rule out any psychiatric issues due to seeing and interacting with spirits in their homes. When they were cleared by the doctor, they called us to figure out the next step to understanding and knowing what was going on. We don't ask clients to do this, but I try to rule out everything that may be happening in a home or to a client. Not everything is paranormal and people should seek out all options to help themselves in any way to get better.

Psychological Issues

Some people that I have investigated for tell me that they have other issues going on besides paranormal ones, and I try to determine what is best for dealing with their issues. This is hard for a person to talk about, but many times, he or she does open up to me, so I listen and try to turn them in the right direction.

Many people are labeled as schizophrenic for hearing voices or seeing things. I don't always think this is a mental health issue as I know some people are just sensitive and can see and hear things others cannot.

While investigating, I look into what they are telling me and what they are experiencing in the home to see if there is any truth to it and if any evidence can be found. I leave it up to them to contact therapists if they want to get professional help. Sometimes, it can be a combination of past traumas and paranormal issues going on. It gets complicated and that is where professional help is also needed. If they are having sleep issues such as sleep paralysis, the condition of being unable to move while in bed, the dreams they do have can be so realistic that they feel they are real. It's really hard to tell if what they are experiencing is actually real or not.

Many people do have dreams connected to the spirits when there is paranormal activity going on in their home. I do sometimes think it can be related to the haunting, but it's really hard to tell. The only way to find out if someone has sleep paralysis is to give them a sleep test. A doctor will monitor a person to see if there are any issues while sleeping. It's impossible for me to determine what is really happening until the client gets tested and other possibilities, including other reasons why they having issues at night, have been ruled out.

Many people say of clients like this, "Well, it's only in their heads and they're having illusions." However, that's not always the case. I have people tell me things that I have later caught as evidence or that really existed at some point in time. Another issue would be that they are experiencing extreme headaches or having extremely high anxiety. Again, it's something you have to figure out and try to explain. Sometimes, it's the house and the electrical units giving off extremely high amounts of EMFs or people sleeping next to electrical boxes or wiring that may be damaged or wired wrongly. This is where the hard work comes in because we need to rule out all areas which might be affecting these people in their home. These include what is causing the issues and how these issues can be resolved to keep the areas safe for the occupants.

The anxiety may be something only a doctor can fix. At other times, it may be that the client just needs what is happening around him or her to be fixed. In one case, a man was having blurred vision because he believed he was trying to block out the bad energy he was feeling in his home, and what was going on around him. The energy was very bad there. I could also feel the high energy in an old building nearby his house. The building had very high EMF energy spikes, and there were static lights going off and on in it. Although there was a high amount of activity in the home, it was not the cause of his poor eyesight. He got his eyes checked and he only needed glasses, so his health situation was not connected to the paranormal activity in their home. That is why it is important to investigate all natural events or health issues and not just paranormal things going on. If things still do not get better, the people should possibly see a trained person such as a psychiatrist or doctor and try to get some professional help. Not everything is paranormal. That is why it's important to keep an open mind.

Portals

When investigating haunted places, we do find there are portals that seem to be in a home. I often ask the psychic why there is a lot of activity or where it's coming from. One medium said, "Look here and feel this wall." So I put my hand over the area where she pointed to and felt the wall. I was shocked to experience very cold air coming out of the area. I usually go into debunking mode and look for natural causes or what may be causing the cold air effect when it happens. Many times, I haven't been able to debunk this. However, when the medium was done clearing the room, the cold air coming from the wall had disappeared. It actually changed to warm air and the wall really felt warm, which was very strange. Using a temperature gauge, I documented that the air in the room changed 6-15 degrees within the time the medium cleared the bad energy and closed the portal in the room. I thought it was interesting to actually document that the room temperature did change with scientific data. You could feel the energy lighten up and a calming feeling can be felt in the room.

I asked where the portals came from. One medium said, "They can be created from sensitive children in the home and they do not even realize they did this." After children have the ability and energy to do this, some portals are created in other ways which are not good. Different spirits can come through these portals and travel back and forth. Sometimes, bad spirits or entities who are not good, use the portals to enter people's houses. The owners usually say, "Well it felt okay, but one week, we felt something really negative here. We are not sure why." When people experience so much activity with different spirits, sometimes there is a portal somewhere in the home that needs to be closed.

Dreams

Many people tell me about their dreams that they have. Some are scary, some are premonitions and some are connected to the haunting they may be dealing with in their home. I have had people tell me they had a dream about something, and it actually happened to them a week later. They thought it was only a dream, but in a sense, they had a vision of what would happen to them in the future. They were shocked when this dream became a reality. I believed they had some form of psychic ability.

Another part of the phenomena was that their dream was connected to activity happening in their home. One lady said she "dreamed of a little boy with blond hair." He was talking to her and running around her bed. She also had activity in her house and heard children playing in her home. What really got her was when I had a psychic medium read her house. The medium said, "You know, you have a little boy here. He has blond hair and is about 6 years old."

The lady freaked out and said, "Oh my God! That's the little boy I have been dreaming about all the time here."

I do believe that when we are asleep, we're very open, relaxed, and more receptive to spirit communication, so it makes sense that spirits might try to communicate when this happens. I have had many people tell me they have had dreams of spirits, and even whole families of spirits, in their homes. One lady said, "I had dreams of this family living here in my home. One night, the family of spirits seemed upset and they told me in my dream they'd had enough and were moving out." After that dream, she never again experienced any activity in her home.

The lady said, "The spirits must've really left my home 'cause I never had any more dreams or activity here after that." I thought that pretty interesting.

Provoking Spirits

When I first got into investigating homes, I tried provoking spirits. I did not realize what I was doing or the consequences of what might happen because I was making them mad. One night, we were investigating a very old barn in the middle of the night. The lady of the home had reported that she was experiencing disturbances from someone who had died there. We were challenging them to make themselves known to us through some sort of physical act. My brother even dared one of them to push him. Suddenly, all of my batteries were drained out completely.

This happens on investigations quite a lot. The theory is that the spirits use the energy from the batteries. That is why the batteries are drained of life. The energy gives the entities or spirits strength so they can become more powerful. They can also consume energy from phones and other devices that are powered with any type of battery.

When the batteries drained down in my equipment, I thought something might happen there so I quickly went out to my car to get fresh ones. When I was at my car, the other investigator who had been provoking the spirits heard some footsteps walking behind him. At first, he thought it was me. He soon realized it was not me, but a spirit walking behind him. The footsteps got closer. He called out to me to see if I would answer him. No one called back to him, but the footsteps kept getting closer and closer. Then all of sudden, they were right behind him. As he turned to take a picture, something which felt like a finger poked him really hard in the middle of the back. He jumped up and turned around, but did not see anyone.

We realized then that provoking spirits was not a great idea, and we stopped after that night. I would advise against doing what we did in this situation. We learned our lesson when it comes to provoking spirits, and hope that others refrain as well.

Telekinesis

The sensitivity of some people seems to attract different paranormal activities in their home. They do not realize that it's actually their own energy causing these phenomena. What I mean by this is that they can actually move things telekinetically and cause other strange activity to occur with their own energy. Some people have the natural ability to do this and do not even know it. If you have ever watched a person bending spoons or moving objects around without physically touching them, this can be very amazing. I have seen this with table tipping: people put their hands on the table and cause the table to move or tip with their energy, without using the strength of their hands/bodies. The same is true in a home in which objects seemingly move by themselves: doors open and close, dishes thrown. One lady even had an air conditioner lid rise off the air conditioner and fly across the room. The people in homes like this are terrified of these events and do not realize that they may be the ones creating these with their own energy.

Past Lives /Reincarnation

I have heard some stories from different people that seem to agree with the theory of reincarnation. I do believe in past lives. When we die, we can come back here to earth and relive another life. Some say that while we are here on earth, we have certain life-learning goals to achieve. If we do not learn from these goals, we repeat our life until we get it right. It's like the saying, "They are old souls." It comes from living many lives and learning from them. How it is that children can know different languages at very young ages or they can sit down and play instruments without ever learning how to play? I believe they know how to do this from a previous life and brought this knowledge over with them into this life. Bits and pieces come along from previous lives and can even affect us when this happens. Some might be afraid of heights or water, or have other phobias. When they have these fears, I believe they may have fallen off a very high building or drowned in a past life. That scary event can impact us and imprint on our soul as it is relived here on earth.

There are people that do past life regression and take clients back through previous lives lived. Sometimes, this helps the people get through the phobias they are having, and let go of their previous issues held over from their past life/lives. One person told me a story of losing one of her family members from a suicide. The same time her sister died of the suicide, she found out that she was pregnant. When her daughter was only a few years old, the little girl started saying that her name was "Sara," a name which was not the name that her mother had chosen to give her. Well, Sara was the name of the sister who had committed suicide. The young girl also pointed to the calendar and said, "That's my birthday on the calendar." The date she pointed to was actually the mother's sister, Sara's, birthday.

The mother started to wonder how the little girl knew Sara's very important dates, such as her birthday. The little girl also had very blue eyes just like Sara's, and even some of Sara's personality traits. It made the mother nervous that the daughter knew personal things that a little girl should not know. They found out later that they lived in a home in which another young girl had taken her life. They would often see the little spirit girl and had so many experiences that they ended up moving. It's weird because the girl had also taken her life in the same bedroom her daughter was staying in. It was all too much for the mother, as she started to wonder why this all happened. After a few years, the daughter did not say much more about her sister, Sara, and everything seemed to be okay. It bothered the mother though as she could not figure out why this all happened. I have to say that it was intriguing that so many different scenarios seemed connected to the sister's death.

Earth-bound Spirits

Some spirits stay earth-bound for different reasons such as a passing of a relative or a very traumatic event during which a person never gets to say goodbye" to their loved ones. I have seen many things which seem to cause activity, from suicides and tragic car accidents right down to serious health reasons. Again, this is all in theory and from what I have witnessed during investigations in different homes and while interacting with psychic mediums. If a person dies and does not want to cross over, the idea that he or she would continue on in this world would make sense. After working with many intuitive and psychic people, I do see this with suicides, possible murders, and unexplained or unexpected deaths.

Some spirits seem to be emotional, either angry or sad.

You can actually sense this when you walk into a house. Other mediums have told me that some spirits can cross from one dimension to the other. They travel back to earth and make contact because the spirits felt that they needed to either protect a family member, or just try to give them an important message to clear some unfinished business. The other reason why the spirits were there was because someone in the house was very sensitive.

There are different scenarios which play out, so being very open to different types of hauntings helps. I do think that much of the activity which has happened in homes has involved family spirits who had been trying to get the family's attention. The other investigations were for other reasons, and some of them were quite scary. The latter were usually connected to a ritual, Ouija Board session, or some type of cult, or situation a person dabbled in.

People can open up a portal or stir up energy which results in a negative haunting without realizing what they have done until it is too late. That is usually when I get a phone call. It always starts off with something like this: "You are going to think I'm crazy and you are not going to believe what is going on here." It is usually in a very nervous, low tone. These people have no one else to turn to, so I get a very long story about what has happened to them in their home. I like hearing their stories not just because it is what I do, but because I usually have an idea of what is going on there, unless they leave out some parts they do not want to tell me. I usually get the whole story at some point though.

Objects can hold onto energy

After investigating many homes and places I have noticed that objects can hold onto past energy. I have documented this many times. Items such as dolls, old clocks, and even clothes can hold energy from the past. One case was a doll that was sending very high EMFs off it. My meter would spike as high as 30 and immediately go back to zero. I was shocked to see this but I had seen before that many personal items can still hold very high energy around them. It made me wonder if the person had stayed with the personal item after they passed on or maybe some of the energy imprinted onto the item and stayed with it for many years after they had moved on. I know some items should not be giving out any electrical impulses. This scientifically should not be happening so it has to be something else doing this. I always try to rationalize or debunk things in a scientific matter but sometimes you just can't and that's where you have to look at it in a different perspective and know energy is around an object for some reason.

Here is a very old dress in a museum that I had investigated. As I sat next to the dress I noticed my EMF meter would spike and then go back to zero. The meter was on a table right next to the dress so I held my meter up next to the dress and was shocked to see very high EMFs around the old piece of clothing. I realized there must be some sort of energy still clinging onto the dress. I also wondered if this was the reason for some of the activity in the museum.

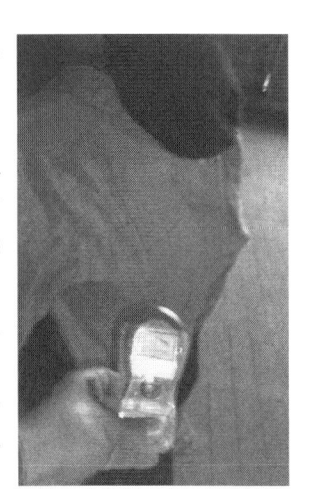

Native Americans

Many cases I have worked on seemed connected to the Native American culture in some way. Please note that there are many different tribes and cultures within the Native American population so it is hard to generalize. Many people with a Native American cultural background that I have engaged with seem to have a higher awareness and openness to the paranormal. Given that many Native American cultures seems to be spiritually aware, it does make sense that people with these cultures inherit that very openness, pick up on spirits, and draw a certain amount of energy and activity to themselves. Some people are very empathic and others, being gifted, have psychic abilities. One man was watching me use my dowsing rods. He said, "I'm pretty skeptic of that." He thought I was moving them with my hands.

I said, "Why don't you then try the dowsing rods and see what happens?" He picked the dowsing rods up and soon, as he held them out, they started moving really fast. The man actually dropped the dowsing rods on the floor, because they startled him by actually moving in his hands.

"Holy crap," He yelled. "They really do work! I thought this was all bullshit. I'm an engineer and I work in a factual mode and with a scientific knowledge, not anything like this."

I asked, "Well, what is your heritage or background?"

"Oh, I have a lot of Native American in me. My mom is almost all Native American.

"That makes sense then."

"What does?" the man asked me.

"Native Americans can be very spiritual and have very open spiritual views of the paranormal and often believe in it."

The guy looked up and said, "Well, I believe it now, too. I always thought this was all fake, but now I believe it after seeing it and feeling it."

"That's good, and I bet some of your family members have some stories of their own, too," I replied.

Inhuman and Demonic Entities

Many cases we have worked on are pretty benign or not

harmful to the clients and investigators working on the case. But the smaller 2% of cases that are actually really bad have had much more negative, sickening, or unsettling energies that had the ability to harm people. These cases are a lot different than the normal ones we have investigated.

Sometimes there are warning signs people must be aware of. Usually, when we walk into a place with these negative energies, we get weird, almost edgy, anxious or uneasy feelings in our guts. Sometimes it's just a feeling to it or possibly what the clients may be telling or possibly hiding from you. Other groups may have passed up the case or refused to do it. One case I worked on had a really bad dream about the house before I actually investigated it. It seemed so real I thought I was actually fighting off a very demonic-looking creature. Another investigator had the very same dream I had. They said that they were standing next to me, fighting off some weird-looking, huge, black creature.

During other cases, clients were being harmed. I just got the feeling that the entity was really threatening while walking into the home. The families were scared and did not want to talk about what was happening. Many red flags shoot up and warn the investigators about what they are in for. I never really believed in the hype of demons. I thought the whole thing was made-up for TV and unreal. However, after working on some bad cases, I do believe in bad entities and how they can harm people.

The whole idea of a biblical fallen angel turning into a demon is pretty scary. These bad entities are out to ruin peoples' lives and destroy them. They break up people's relationships by pitting them against each other, messing with their minds and creating stress between them with their actions. They also attack people at night. People can wake up with scratches and bruises on their bodies. One woman was actually held down in her bed by one of these beings. They can also swing open doors and move objects around rooms. Their energy can make people feel physically sick as well.

When dealing with these bad entities, I think it is a battle of good versus evil. I do not think these demonic spirits are anything to mess with if someone does not have the knowledge to handle them or these types of cases. If we do not go in prepared, it can be unsafe to both the investigators and the clients. Investigators should be aware of the dangers and be ready to act every time they go into these cases.

Empathic Abilities

When I say, "empathic," I mean that people can pick up on the feelings of others. If someone is sad, she or he picks up on that. The same goes for spirits around a person. An empathic person or "empath" picks up on another's feelings and emotions. Some people do not realize this and wonder why they go through so many different moods. They need to realize what is happening to them, that they are actually picking up on other peoples' feelings.

I think it's important for the empath to know/realize the difference between the empath's emotions, another person's emotions, or the emotions of a spirit in the area. The empath should also know whether the energy is happening now or if it is residual energy left over from a spirit or persons who are no longer in the space where the feelings are being picked up.

Many people have a natural and normal reaction of empathy to sad or angry emotions, so they will cry or feel upset. However, when a person has the gift of empathy, she or he really feels the emotions and what's around him or her in a magnified way. It can be ten times worse than regular feelings of empathy. Empathic people really need to ground and protect themselves so they don't have to be so affected by others' energies. They need to learn to separate their own feelings and other people's feelings they are picking up.

Electrical Energy

If a spirit wants to give a loved one a message, but no longer has a way to do it, he or she will try to get the owner's attention by doing something. It can be by manipulating electrical or electronic devices and flashing lights off and on. I have heard of spirits making fire alarms go off. I have seen light bulbs explode or pop due to high electrical currents. I have experienced situations in which owners have had phone messages on their phones that could not be explained. Elevators have opened on their own for no discernible reason. I have personally videotaped and witnessed children's toys turning off and on without anyone's manipulation. Again, ghost hunters attempt to debunk or explain all phenomena scientifically. We want to have a rational and concrete explanation for why electrical objects might go off for no reason. However, sometimes you just cannot explain them that way. It makes sense, though, that if a spirit or ghost consists of energy themselves, they should be able to manipulate electrical devices because these objects are powered by, contain, and consist of that same energy.

Residual Energy

When I say I believe its residual energy in a home, people ask me what is residual energy? I have to explain to them how a house can have an imprint of energy from the past. Residual imprints can stay in a home as it is imprinted in the wood and its surroundings. Residual energy can be left over from a very traumatic event or extremely intense situation that may have happened in a home. It is not really there, just left over energy or an imprint in a home that is still there. Most times a residual haunting will repeat the event over and over again. It's almost like a time warp and it just replays itself over and over. It is usually harmless because the ghosts are not really there. It is just left over energy from many years ago. I usually ask the owner if they heard or saw the spirit at a certain time. Sometimes similar events replay themselves over and over. Some owners have seen full body apparitions walk up their stairs. It usually happens either once a year or around the same time once a week or month, or every night at the same time.

I usually try to document this at the very time the owner sees or witnessed the apparition on the stairs. If it is residual it's usually happens at the same time. The other thing that usually happens is there is no communication between the spirit and the homeowners. When I ask what the spirit did or acted like when they walked past the homeowner, they stated the spirit did not see them or even look at them and just walked right by them like they were not there. This usually tells me the spirit was actually residual energy and just an imprint in time and not really there. It is still scary for the homeowner though and quite unnerving. It is been said that houses have been completely demolished and new homes built over the same area. The same activity happens because it is residual and probably connected to the land not the house. For instance, if ghosts are seen walking through walls, that may be because there was not a wall in that location when the imprint took hold so it is walking the path through its old house instead of the new. I always find these stories fascinating and how energy can carry on for many years.

Intelligent Energy

The next thing I try to do is get an intelligent response from a spirit. If I ask if a spirit is there in a home and I get a yes in a response to my question on my recorder, I would start to think it may be an intelligent haunting. That usually means that the spirit is there and can hear and interact with you and they know what is happening in the home. Many times a spirit still thinks they still own their home and they really never left this world. The spirit is living in a different realm but in the same house and carrying on with their same activities they did when they were alive. I believe that is one of the main reasons a spirit in a home can get upset over any changes or any repairs to the home and cause chaos in a home if they don't like what is going on there. One lady told me she was wallpapering and something seemed to be pulling the wallpaper out of her hands as she tried to add new wallpaper. "I guess they did not want that kind of wallpaper so I stopped wallpapering." she said. I am always fascinated what type of energy spirits can display when they want to. Many people are skeptics until something very unusual happens to them they cannot explain.

Animals Are Sensitive

It is interesting to see a dog or cat look at a corner or have their hair stand straight up on their backs or just freak out when no one is around them. A couple of times they would stand at the top of the stairs and look down at the basement and refuse to even go near it. I do feel it is best to keep the animals out of a home while investigating. Having an animal in a home while investigating also adds contamination to evidence and it is harder to tell if it is paranormal or not. Animals usually will warn you if there is a presence in a home. They can be good indicators that a spirit may be in a home. I do not think that it is fair to the animal to have them in a home while investigating. I have seen pets start going crazy while we were investigating a home. One dog was in a dog crate and starting biting at the cage very fiercely. The owners put the dog outside and it started digging at the front door to get back in the house. The owners were amazed because their dog was usually calm and never acted that way. I have seen cats act very strangely too and just staring in areas like they were seeing something standing there. Many cases we have seen animal spirits come through, too. We have even collected EVPs of a dog barking in a very old abandoned house.

Skeptics

I usually like skeptics, as I want actual proof or evidence of a haunted location. Many times, I can debunk noises and rule out supposed paranormal activities in a home. I have to laugh though because the skeptics usually are the ones that experience the most activity around them. One lady journalist laughed at us and said, "I'm 98 percent skeptic and never have believed in this stuff."

I just laughed and I actually said, "Well, the skeptics usually have something happen to them."

The lady became a little nervous, "Well, not me! I have never seen or felt anything."

"Well, have you ever been in a haunted location?"

She had nothing to say to that.

Later in the night, the lady was helping us out as I dowsed and got some energy right where she was standing. The lady was holding an EMF meter in her hand. When her face started to get agitated, the lady said, "What the? The meter is going way up. I feel like something is going on. "The lady became instantly agitated and started to show a very scared look on her face.

About the same time, she started to get physically thrown backwards. "Ouch!" she yelled, "Oh, hell no!" And she started running downstairs very quickly. No one was near her and we could see her body actually lunge backwards. The lady quickly ran down the steps mumbling something like, "I don't want to be here!"

We found out later that the lady was hit in her chest, sending her backwards and she had the bruises to prove it. She turned into a believer after that night, so be careful about what you say because skeptics become easy targets for ghosts. I like to think the ghosts have more to prove to the skeptics. The reaction to being pushed or picked on is priceless. Not that I want to see anyone get hurt or harmed during an investigation. I like the fact people get proven wrong when they go in with a skeptical attitude.

Astral Travel

I have always been curious about astral travel and how certain people can do this. Some of the people I know who can astral travel tell me their stories. They tell me after I fall asleep that I can drift out of my body and travel to other locations. One lady said she was floating over her body while she was asleep. "I could clearly see myself lying in my bed as I drifted high above it. It's a weird sensation." she said.

Some people seem to travel to other locations or dimensions while they are asleep. Some feel a heavy feeling pushing down on their chest. They believe it's their spiritual body going back in their physical body. Some mediums get messages while in their deep dream state of sleep, too. One medium thought she had crossed over to the Other Side and received messages from angels in a heaven-like setting.

Remote Viewing

Some psychics can use remote viewing when they want to see something in a different location. Sometimes they see things connected to my paranormal cases. One psychic started to tell me what the owners looked like at the location we were going to and what was going on in the home. "Oh, I see two little girls living in the home." she said. "One has large eyes and shoulder-length, brown hair and wears large glasses. She is quite talkative too, and likes the activity there. She is open and gifted to this." she said. "The other girl is very shy and hides behind the legs of her mother sometimes. She doesn't say much because she is very shy."

"You got it right." I said, "That's amazing!" I knew she did not even know where we were going, let alone any names of the people there at this house. I usually do not tell the psychics anything while going to these locations, so it's unlikely that they know what any of the ghosts or spirits look like, or even about the personalities that they see. One medium texted me and starting telling me what the inside and outside of the house looked like that I was investigating. She said, "You are investigating right now; I see the house. Oh, a spirit girl is there and she stands at the bottom of the stairs." the medium said. "That's where she plays with the light switch, opens the gate on the stairs, and lets the dogs go up."

I showed the owners the texts from the psychic medium. They were surprised that anyone could do this. Their gate was opened all the time and the light switch by the stairs would switch on by itself. The medium had seen everything that had been happening there through remote viewing.

Shadow People

Some of my investigations include people seeing shadow figures in their home. It's quite scary and I have seen them myself while investigating homes. The first time I had seen a shadow figure, it was in a very old asylum. All three of the investigators saw two small shadow figures walk by. It's hard to wrap your mind around it. We try to process what we are seeing, but still don't believe it, at least in my opinion. I have a very scientific background when investigating and can usually debunk many things happening in a home. But, when you see a shadow figure, it's hard to take in and process what you are seeing. The second time, three different investigators saw the shadow figure walk down a hallway and into a bedroom. I did a double take, then walked down to the room to make sure that the ghost wasn't really a living person down by the bedroom. When I looked inside the bedroom, no one was there. It was hard to believe what I was seeing was real. I have videotaped shadow people and have actual evidence they do exist. This is why we set so many video cameras up so we can have real proof of their existence. When showing the people what I had captured on video they were overwhelmed. They actually said that's what we had seen in the back of the old theater and watched the shadow figure walk by them. They could not believe I had caught it on my video. At the same time they were delighted that they had really seen a ghost!

The next questions people ask me are, "Why shadow people? Why are they here? What do they want from us?" The latter is the million dollar question and I wish I could totally answer it. The only way I can reply is that they don't all seem negative in my dealings with them. In some cases, there were some negative situations with the shadow people but not all of them. In a real haunting, a lot of times, shadow people are seen. I thought at first the shadow people may be observers during a haunting. While at other times, a tragic event had occurred and they were also there. That's why it's hard for me to put them in one category because I have seen them in different scenarios.

Some people think because they are dark shadows that they are automatically bad and they want to harm you. I don't think this is always the case though. I have seen some negative things around shadow people but I can't say that is why they are in a home. Saying, "It's evil and demonic," is wrong. Way too many people categorize this and say, "They are demons." I think this is wrong and it just scares the family even more. Fear feeds activity in a home and this is the last thing you want to do to a family if they are experiencing paranormal activity. Have I worked on bad cases? Yes, I have, but you only see a few bad cases while investigating. Maybe one or two out of 100 cases will you run into something really negative. I think the whole demon thing is wrong because it just scares people more and creates more problems in a home. The last thing you want to do to a family is frighten them even more than they are already.

The only other conclusion to me is that a shadow person is dark because it doesn't have enough energy to fully form itself. I'm on the fence with that explanation. I have had people tell me that they watched a dark mist while it formed into a shape of a person. This still does not mean it's not harmful, but it makes you wonder what kind of energy it was taking on. Is it fooling people by taking on a person-like form? This is why it's important to keep an open mind and not rush to conclusions and sometimes it is really hard to say for sure what it truly is. That's why I say, "It's only in theory," because that's all we can really say. The proof is still not out there yet on shadow people. Some mediums will tell you differently, as well as other investigators. Every person's opinion matters and no one is really wrong because we don't totally know for sure what shadow people are.

Talking with Skeptics Out There

I like it when people say that they are skeptics and don't believe in ghosts. When people say, "Well, I'm skeptical about ghosts and have a hard time believing in that stuff," usually further down in our conversation, they'll tell me about an experience they have had involving ghosts. I can't say whether or not their experience was real or really happened, but because I've had my own experiences, I can't disbelieve them. They'll say, "I saw my grandfather standing by my bed after he had passed on. He looked at me and said something like, 'I love you. It's okay.' But it wasn't real, even though I thought I was awake and sitting-up, looking at him. I thought it was my brain playing tricks on me or something because I could never see ghosts. They were all just unreal; a big illusion or something."

As I listen to people talk themselves out of some pretty cool experiences, I realize they are trying to rationalize what happened to them and just writing it off as something they made up or thought in their minds. I usually say, "But what if it was true and you really did see your grandfather standing by your bed and it really did happen? It's not really scary, actually. I think it's cool you got a message from him."

Then they say, "Well, I guess, but I don't want ghosts around me and don't like what happened to me."

"Oh, you had other experiences, too?"

"Yes, but I don't like talking about them."

When I hear this, I know they are just trying to protect themselves and trying to stay closed- off to the spirit world. They are not skeptics at all, really; they want to tell me their stories and see how I react to make sure that I don't think they are crazy. Some people open up and tell me even more stories, saying, "Well, it's not that I'm really that skeptical. I believe in it. I just don't want people thinking I'm in the loony bin or something."

I almost have to laugh because I usually know where this conversation is leading, too. I get to hear more of their stories if I accept them as sane because they know what I do. When I say to them, "Yes, other people have had that happen to them, too. It's not just you." They seem to get a little closure by talking about it.

Near Death Experiences

Some people say it is very close to an out of body experience when they have a Near Death Experience or NED. Some skeptics say, "Well, it's just electrical impulses in the brain still working after death." Well, if your blood is not flowing and the brain is not receiving oxygen, I wonder how people could interpret and even remember certain events while they were laying lifeless on an operating table or somewhere else. One person even remembered the instruments the doctor was using when they were operating on him as he was dying on the table. Another person remembered some bits of her family's conversation while she was lifeless on the operating table. Some people could feel themselves floating over their lifeless body while clinically dead. They knew they had died and seen the rescue workers trying to revive them. Some even crossed over and had seen and even spoke to deceased family members.

I do not think this would be possible if these patients were clinically dead and not able to see or hear what was going on at the time. There has to be more to this than "electrical surges going through the body still." The same goes for people who went into comas and woke up unexpectedly. Some mediums say, "We are half on this side and half on the other side while in a coma state."

Some coma patients even responded to people around them. It makes you wonder though as modern day science is starting to prove that the brain is far more advanced than we know it to be. I think we have come a long way from burning so-called witches at the stake and are now actually opening up our minds and knowing that there is much more out there than we can see or feel.

Children Are Very Sensitive

Children are very open to the paranormal and to the spirits. Many people think it's because the children have not been conditioned to this physical world yet and are open to the spiritual world. As kids get older, they are taught not to believe in the intangible, just grow older and less sensitive.

There have been cases in which children seem to be sensing or seeing spirits and/or having interactions with spirits. At times, the parents had heard their children playing in a room and interacting with someone. They could hear their children's voices and hear another voice speaking to them on a home baby monitor device. One of the children had been rolling a ball to some unseen force and the ball would roll back to the child, seemingly on its own. The child had said something like, "The little boy is here," or, "I'm playing with a little girl in my room."

As you can imagine, listening to someone talk to their children who wasn't there when the parents walked into the room was quite scary for the parents.

Of course the parents had said, "It's an imaginary friend." Other parents in similar situations have fabricated some kind of excuse as to why these situations had happened. In most cases like these, the children involved outgrew these experiences as their senses weakened. In some cases, I believe the children who were spirits or ghosts were drawn to the living children in a home. In most of these cases, the children were unharmed, but some children were frightened and refused to sleep in their own rooms at night. Most of the time, it is possible to ask the spirits not to harm or mess with the children. That often works to keep the living children from experiencing spirit communication or activities. After all, spirits were once human and they usually get the point if you are firm with them. Sometimes a psychic medium needs to come to the home to help a spirit move on by sending them to the light. Not all spirits are nice and it takes some work to encourage them to leave.

Possession

While doing seminars, people ask me about being taken over by some force that you cannot see. I tell them that I have had my experiences of seeing people possessed. It is scary and it *can* happen. When I first got into this Paranormal field, I thought that possession was only a movie hoax and therefore unreal. Now, I have to say that it is real, and that people need to be careful while investigating and doing this kind of work.

I was investigating a very old abandoned home with a psychic medium. She mentioned that she would open herself up more that night and asked me to just watch her to make sure that if she acted differently due to a spirit taking over her body to help out. "Can they do that?" I asked.

"Yes, if I let them." the medium said, "Spirits can jump into your body and take over. I don't like that and do not usually let spirits do that." she said.

"If I see anything happen or you act differently I will help you out." I said.

Later, during the investigation of the same old abandoned home, the medium said, "Oh there is a real angry guy in this room here with us."

I said, "That's not good."

Another medium picked up the same energy in the room, too. She said she thought he may have killed a woman by throwing her down the stairway. It made me think of the spirit voices arguing, which I had caught on tape earlier in the same home. The conversation was between a woman and a man. The woman was yelling at the man while the man was beating the woman up. Heard on tape were noises which sounded like slaps, hits, and bumps. At the end, there was a loud "thud" noise, as if someone had abruptly fallen down. This was followed by a loud, crashing sound. This was recorded while the other psychic was picking-up on the angry feeling from a spirit man there.

The psychic next to me started acting weirdly. This medium is usually very calm and mild-mannered. However, at that moment, I noticed her walking very forcefully away and stomping around. Her fists were clenched and her face was very tense. The medium looked down the hallway and started screaming, "That boy better get back in his room!"

"Holy shit! What is going on?" I exclaimed. No one seemed to notice the strange behavior of the medium. I walked closer to her to try to help. When I got close to her, I could see the medium's face change right in front of me. It started to elongate and was very scary looking. "Holy shit!" I yelled. "We need to get her out of this house now!"

The medium started to stumble toward the stairs. I ran over to stop her and quickly turned her around, away from the steep stairway. Whatever was possessing her seemed to be taking her down the steep stairway as a way to hurt the medium by making her fall down the stairs. I grabbed her and steered her the right way out of the house. When we got outside, the medium looked at me and asked, "What happened? Where am I?"

She did not remember any of the things that happened in the house. "I think you were taken over by the angry guy there." I said. The psychic looked very angry and I thought she was going to punch me in the face so I kept my distance for a few minutes. The medium quickly put her hands and feet on the ground and tried to ground herself to get rid of the negative energy she was feeling inside her still.

The medium later told me that it had taken weeks to rid herself of the negative and very angry energy she was feeling. It is something I will never forget. I have learned that people had better be careful while investigating extremely haunted places.

While sometimes a possession can be bad, I have also heard of stories in which people were possessed, but for them, it was not a bad thing. Here is another story I heard from one lady, connected to what I would call a possession:

The police called and asked me to stop down at the police station to make a statement. "Whatever for?" I responded back.

"You do not remember what happened last night?" the police officer said.

"No, I don't. Can you please tell me what happened and why you want me to come to the police station?"

"Well, we got a phone call from you about 2 in the morning last night," the officer said. "You told us a robbery was in progress at the jewelry store, just down the street from you. When we responded to the call, you were standing outside by the street and pointing at the jewelry store just down the road from you. You were wearing your pajamas and looked wide awake." the officer said. "When we arrived at the jewelry store, we actually found a man robbing the store and arrested him. Your call helped us catch this man and prevented him from getting away with it. If you cannot remember anything, we probably have enough evidence from catching him in the act. Thanks for your help and have a nice day."

The lady told me she never remembered any of it and thought she had been sleeping all night. However, the police had clearly seen her standing in front of her own home and documented the phone call from the woman at her house. After listening to this, I just shook my head and thought, "Wow! What a cool story. Ghosts help stop a crime by taking over another person's body."

This possession seemed harmless, but not all possessions are as easy and fun as that one was. I do believe that whether a human spirit, ghost, or some other entity takes over a person, whoever it is can be good or bad. The possessed is usually someone who is very open to the spirit world and who can very easily channel spirits. The person's openness makes it easier for spirits to take him or her over.

Inviting Danger

Sometimes, the owner is drawing the activity in a home and actually inviting a spirit or spirits there for different reasons. This is usually not a good thing and forms of attachments can occur. It's not a good thing as it can turn into a very bad situation. This usually happens when a device is used such as an Ouija Board or séances or rituals are done. When you are opening yourself up to something that you don't realize who or what you are dealing with it can be dangerous. I always tell people to be careful when practicing rituals or using devices such as Ouija boards. I inform them it's dangerous and not to do it. I personally stay away from doing this and keep the White Light of protection around me at all times.

Personal Protection

Many people ask me if they can protect themselves or remove negative energy in a home. I say, "Yes. There are things you can do for yourself to make you feel better in your home." For example, if you are moving into an apartment or new home, you can cleanse it first. Maybe you feel you need some negative energy lifted in your current home. You can clear the negative energy left behind by smudging your home. This goes back to Native American cultures due to their spiritual ways. Usually, they burn sage to smudge with to protect themselves. Some people like the cedar and sage, while others use sweet grass to promote positive feelings and please the spirits. You can use both sage and sweet grass if you want to. Many times, a medium will clear the negative energy in a home by smudging a home. I think that's the best way to go due to the medium's abilities. The sage works together with the medium to clear up the energy. I usually feel the effects of the smudging right away. The rooms feel lighter and there aren't any heavy feelings in the rooms anymore after a smudging by a medium. More religious people may want to have a house blessing done by their local church. I think you should use whatever is correct for your belief if that will work for you. Someone taught me to soak cedar in holy water and then use the holy water in a spray bottle. When a person feels negative energy around him or her, he or she can spray the area around him or her to feel protected.

Again: Whatever works for you, I would use. Some like medallions and wear them around their necks. It's something you can have with you at all times.

Some ask for protection by surrounding themselves

with white light. I also use this method of protection. If you are very open or sensitive, you might also have to ground and shield yourself. When you ground yourself, you should concentrate and envision having a beam of white light around and within you. Start at your head and work the light downwards to your feet. Have the light push any negative energy through your body and into the ground. You want to push the bad energy into the ground and deep down almost like roots going down deep into the ground.

After you ground yourself, you will want to protect yourself with white light. Visualize a white light shield around you. The shield is almost like a bubble, so nothing negative can harm you when the white light is surrounding you. Some say that bringing in positive energy into a home by cleaning, painting, and just airing out old energy works too.

Protection Prayers

The Lord's Prayer

"Our father, who art in heaven, hallowed be thy name. Thy kingdom come, thy will be done on earth as it is in heaven. Give us this day our daily bread and forgive us our trespasses as we forgive those who trespass against us. And lead us not into temptation, but deliver us from evil. For thine is the kingdom and the power and the glory, forever. Amen."

Prayer to Saint Michael

"Saint Michael the Archangel, defend us in battle. Be our protection against the wickednesses and snares of the devil. May God rebuke him, we humbly pray. And do Thou, o Prince of the Heavenly Host, by the power of God, thrust into Hell, Satan and all evil spirits who wander throughout the world seeking the ruin of souls. Amen

CONCLUSION

I want to thank you for taking the time to read this book. People do not realize how much time and energy goes into my field. It takes countless hours going over evidence from investigations. If you are a thrill-seeker and are just looking for weekend fun, by all means get involved; here are many places you can go to and investigate. If you are serious, looking to help families out by trying to capture real evidence and figure out what is really going on in a home, then that is great, too.

I really enjoy helping people out to get some closure and calm the activity in a home. I try to be considerate of the family and always remember that my team and I are invited into the family's home to help them out. I understand they are nervous and that having people walk around in someone's home can be intrusive so I always try to remember that while investigating private homes. It's a privilege that people let us into their homes, so I never want to disrespect that in any way. I never thought that I would be doing so many investigations or having so many people call us in to try to help them resolve their paranormal issues.

It amazes me that some people still do not believe in ghosts. We have real ghost photos and videos that back up our claim that ghosts really do exist. That was my first intent: to prove to people that ghosts do exist out there and that there is more than this physical world that we can see or feel. It's even more rewarding to help people out who feel they are alone because there is no one to help them. When their ghostly situation is bad, they pick up the phone and call us. You can also find us on Facebook under Ghost Hunters of the Finger Lakes.

ABOUT THE AUTHOR

Peter Kanellis was born and raised in Brooktondale, NY. He has lived happily with his wife in Lansing, NY for the past 30 years. Together they raised two children who are now married and living nearby with their respective spouses. Peter has worked as a mechanic, in maintenance, and as a youth counselor in his life. This is his first experience with writing. Peter co-founded the Ghost Hunters of the Finger Lakes in 2007.

SPECIAL ACKNOWLEDGEMENTS

While investigating many homes with paranormal activity, I usually run into issues where I need a psychic medium to come to the home. They can help families out by clearing the negative energy from their homes. Thank you to the psychic mediums who have guided me along the way, helped with investigations, and provided closure to families.

One medium I ask to do this is Lorna Reynolds. Every home I have her go to, she seems to hone in on the issues and knows what to do to help the families out. It does not take Lorna long as she sometimes starts telling me what she perceives as early as the car ride there. She tells me details like how many people live in the home, where the activity is or what is happening in the home. She even picks up on the personalities of the people that live there. I am always amazed by her abilities and what she sees before knowing any of my cases.

What I like best is Lorna can help the families get some closure either by telling the families something they need to hear for closure or just explaining why the activity is happening in their homes. I usually get some kind of physical evidence to go along with Lorna's perceptions and advice.

The last and final thing Lorna does is cleanse the home of the negative energy or entities in the home. If she knows that the negative entity is causing the problem, then Lorna gets rid of them.. The activity usually stops after she cleanses the home and the families can finally have some much needed peace and sleep. After she cleanses the home you can actually feel the difference right away. The lingering bad energy is swept away. Thank you, Lorna, for the service and support you provide families during our investigations.

The Open Door

Ms. Lorna Marie Reynolds
Certified Hypnotist * Metaphysical Specialist * Psychic Medium

Making Positive Life Changes Within The Realm Of Time
Private Appointments Seminars, Lectures, Events
thehypnosister@gmail.com
Call and Book Today 1-315-224-8006

Printed in Great Britain
by Amazon